WEIGHTS AND MEASURES   FORMULAS FOR METRIC CONVERSION

To Change	To	Multipy by
liters	gallons (U. S.)	00.26
liters	pecks	00.11
liters	pints (dry)	1.82
liters	pints (liquid)	2.11
liters	quarts (dry)	.91
liters	quarts (liquid)	1.06
ounces	grams	28.35
ounces	pounds	.06

To Change	To	Multiply by
pints (dry)	liters	.55
pints (liquid)	liters	.47
pounds	ounces	16.00
quarts (dry)	liters	1.10
quarts (liquid)	liters	.95
grams	ounces	.035
pounds	grams	453.50
pounds	kilograms	.45
cups	liters	.24

DRY INGREDIENTS

Ounces	Grams
1	28.35
2	56.70
3	85.05
4	113.40
5	141.75
6	170.10
7	198.45
8	226.80
9	255.15
10	283.50
11	311.85
12	340.20
13	368.55
14	396.90
15	425.25
16	453.60

Grams	Ounces
1	0.035
2	0.07
3	0.11
4	0.14
5	0.18
6	0.21
7	0.25
8	0.28
9	0.32
10	0.35
11	0.39
12	0.42
13	0.46
14	0.49
15	0.53
16	0.57

Pounds	Kilograms
1	0.45
2	0.91
3	1.36
4	1.81
5	2.27
6	2.72
7	3.18
8	3.63
9	4.08
10	4.54

Kilograms	Pounds
1	2.21
2	4.41
3	6.61
4	8.82
5	11.02
6	13.23
7	15.43
8	17.64
9	19.84
10	22.05

To
Mary Ann,

THE BUFFALO COOKBOOK

Enjoy! With the
Cooking with the
Healthy Red
Meat ~
great to Meet
you too !!

Fond Regards,
Ruth Mossok Johnston
David Micall Johnston ~

THE BUFFALO COOKBOOK

DEDICATION

My father, Joseph D. Mossok, had many quotes when it came to me (all of which I try to keep ever present in my heart and mind):

> "You can do anything you set your mind to."
> "You never do anything easy or expected."
> "I've always believed you are truly Don Quixote fulfilling the impossible dream."

With this monumental belief and emotional support behind you, how could you possibly lose?

My dad was always right about me. I never did the expected, I never did what was easy, and I always give 150 percent. Eight years ago I lost my father to cancer; eight years ago my husband, David Johnston, had a heart attack; eight years ago my life as I knew it, changed dramatically.

I reflect daily on the love, friendship, and devotion my father and I had for one another. I thank God each day that my husband, who is a wonderful, spiritual inspiration and the love of my life, is still here. For these reasons, I dedicate this book to them.

THE BUFFALO COOKBOOK

THE LOW-FAT, SOLUTION
TO EATING RED MEAT

Ruth Mossok Johnston
Illustrated by David McCall Johnston

hancock

house

ISBN 0-88839-345-8

Cataloging in Publication Data
Johnston, Ruth Mossok, 1951–
     The buffalo cookbook

     ISBN 0-88839-345-8

     1. Cookery (Bison)   I. Title.
TX751.J64 1995   641.6'6292   C95-910634-0

Copy edit: JoAnn Duke
Production: Lorna Brown

Published simultaneously in Canada and the United States by

HANCOCK HOUSE PUBLISHERS LTD.
19313 Zero Avenue, Surrey, B.C. V4P 1M7
(604) 538-1114   Fax (604) 538-2262

HANCOCK HOUSE PUBLISHERS
1431 Harrison Avenue, Blaine, WA 98230-5005
(604) 538-1114   Fax (604) 538-2262

THE BUFFALO COOKBOOK

CONTENTS

6
CONTENTS

THE BUFFALO COOKBOOK

LIST OF ILLUSTRATIONS/PHOTOGRAPHS

8
LIST OF ILLUSTRATIONS/
PHOTOGRAPHS

▲▲▲▲▲▲▲▲▲▲▲▲▲▲▲▲▲▲▲▲▲▲▲▲▲

THE BUFFALO COOKBOOK

ACKNOWLEDGMENTS AND THANKS

▼▼▼▼▼▼▼▼▼▼▼▼▼▼▼▼▼▼▼▼▼▼▼▼▼

The creative process is difficult at best. Without the love, help, and support of many special people, this book would have never become a reality.

My love and thanks to my husband David for being the inspiration, the spiritual strength, and the constant encouragement for this enormous endeavor, as he is in all other aspects of our life. On a professional level, I thank him for his beautiful painting that graces the cover, the powerful graphics that pepper the text, and his input on layout design.

Many thanks to our 13-year-old son Jordan, for his exceptional help in teaching me how to use research equipment at the library, his unconditional love and understanding throughout this time when I was busier than usual with much less quality time for him, and for loving me to pieces none-the-less.

I thank our daughter Kim, and her family, for their love and their understanding—and for helping us celebrate Christmas in February instead of December.

To JoAnn Duke, my dear friend and right hand, endless thanks for her tireless commitment, talent, and assistance in putting this book together...making 2,000,000 manuscript and recipe corrections, pulling "all-nighters" with me (we're definitely too old for this!!) and to her additional commitment to The Johnston Collection. But, most of all, I am grateful for her loyal and sincere friendship that has spanned more than twenty years.

A special thank you to Annabel Cohen, from Annabel's Catering, Southfield, Michigan for her laughter, expertise with food and styling, and for being a great copy editor. She has jumped into this project with both feet and has shown great talent, as well as friendship. An additional thanks to her wonderful staff for their assistance in preparation of the food for the photography shoots.

To Photographers: A heart-felt thanks to Fred Ferris for his beautiful and sensitive photography, for spending long, tiring hours at my house, for having patience with "the team" efforts, and for his commitment to this project. Peyton Mitchell, for her artistic photography and help with this project.

Many Thanks for Photography and/or Props to: The Detroit Institute of Arts, Detroit, Michigan. Magnolia's, Birmingham, Michigan. Mesa Arts, Franklin, Michigan. Barbara Beckwith, Royal Oak, Michigan. Meteor Photo and Imaging, Troy, Michigan. White Reproduction, Inc., Bingham Farms, Michigan. Randazzo's Fruit Market, Detroit, Michigan.

Many Thanks to: Tom Griffith, talented author and historian, for his sensitive and dramatic forward. His insight into the history and plains lifestyle was truly inspiring. Dr. Martin J. Marchello, Professor, Department of Animal and Range Sciences, College of Agriculture, North Dakota State University, for his written contribution and studies on bison meat. Barbara and Don Francis, from Butcher Boy Food Products, Warren, Michigan, for their knowledge and input, and for providing the bison meat for all of the photographs. Florine Mark, President & CEO, Weight Watchers Group, Inc., for her contribution and information related to bison meat.

Thanks to Consultants: Cynthia Rutkowski, R.D., M.A., Clinical Dietitian, Annapolis Hospital, Wayne, Michigan. Brian Mitchell Lee, M.D., Ann Arbor, Michigan. Dr. Robert H. Eckel, M.D., Professor of Medicine and Biochemistry, Biophysics and Genetics, Division of Endocrinology, Department of Medicine, University of Colorado, Health Sciences Center. Marian E. Vorce, R.D., Consultant/Nutritionist, Ypsilanti, Michigan. Patricia Lee, M.A., Lee Bison Meats, Attica, Indiana. Joe Engelhard, M.A., Biologist, Ann Arbor, Michigan. Sandi Folkening, R.N., M.A., Director of Communications, Michigan Heart Association.

Special Thanks to: Kim Dowling, from the former National Buffalo Association, Fort Pierre, South Dakota. Karen Sekich and Gigi Mills from the National Bison Association, Denver, Colorado. Mr. and Mrs. Richard Pohrt, for their generosity in sharing their time, expertise, and precious Native American Artifacts. Dick Pohrt, Jr., for his time and knowledge, and for helping to pull together the necessary Native American items that were needed. Allan Segel, for coming to my computer rescue at all times. And to his wife Diane, for making sure he comes to my computer rescue at all times. Le Creuset of America, Inc., for their generous support and excellent cookware.

To My Personal Friends and Listening Support: Sandra Giachino, Carolyn Jamroz, Tom Crowley, Betty-Lee Sweatt, Kathryn Breech-Raft, Cindy Miner, my cousin Dr. Lisa Ribons, Mildred and Jud Worden, Liz Stamos-Bushey, Sarah Jane Keidan, and Patricia Peart.

10
ACKNOWLEDGMENTS
AND THANKS

THE BUFFALO COOKBOOK

FOREWORD

By T. D. Griffith, Author and Historian

The Lakota brave sat astride his mount surveying a scene of wonder. Stretched before him like the rolling waves of a prairie ocean, the grasslands echoed the rhythms of a ceaseless summer wind, its currents powering the effortless flight of a lone eagle overhead. As the painted pony pawed the gumbo and sniffed the breeze, the Indian scout stared at the valley below. Covering the bluff-bordered plain to the horizon, the largest herd of bison in Dakota Territory stood calmly grazing on belly-high grass.

Cinnamon-colored calves banged heads and rolled in the dirt. The bulls, several weighing more than a ton, ignored the youthful display of energy and instead concentrated on the young shoots of grass just pushing up from the prairie floor. But the Indian, perched on a distant downwind bluff, couldn't see all this. From his vantage, the mass appeared only as a dark blanket cloaking the open range—a migrating commissary of whose flanks his people subsisted. They were in numbers, numberless, and he thanked the Great Spirit—Wakantanka—for His generosity.

The flesh and bones of these great hump-backed beasts would not only feed his people, but would provide them with shelter, clothes, tools, fuel, and a renewed cause for celebration. The hunt would be carefully planned. Upon its success, rode the life of his people.

A silent "surround" was organized. Indians fanned out wide of the herd, slowly, cautiously approaching the buffalo. As they grew nearer, each man quietly lowered himself to the ground and began crawling toward his prey. With a signal, the Indians rose from the grass, screaming, and began running around the startled animals. As the circle was tightened, the hunters gripped their lances and bows and methodically began killing the beasts. As the buffalo on the outside of the circle fell, their bodies formed a roadblock for the living. Soon the circle of dead and dying buffalo had cordoned off any escape for those left alive, and they stood quietly awaiting their certain fate.

When the last buffalo in the circle had been killed, the women joined the bloody task of skinning the animals, slicing strips of meat for drying, and preparing a feast that, when coupled with dancing, would carry on around the campfires into the night in a celebration of life repeated for generations. These animals traveled the grasslands with the stars, the sun, and the wind, often followed by entire tribes, and for centuries it seemed nothing that man could muster could change the drifts of these vast herds.

But by 1870, traditional hunting grounds and a nomadic lifestyle were gradually disappearing for tribes such as the Lakota (Sioux), who once roamed eight million square miles of Midwest prairies and mountain meadows. As white settlement increased and the size of tribal homelands dwindled, so too did their basic food supply—the buffalo. When it was discovered that buffalo hide was ideal for leather goods, hunters flocked to the plains and shot millions of the animals, often leaving their meat for scavenging hawks, eagles, coyotes, and wolves.

By 1889, less than 1,000 buffalo were left in the U.S., and most of those were confined to private herds. Their owners, who were often maligned for clinging to the past, succeeded in rescuing the species from the brink of extinction. Due to the efforts of these few conservationists, today's traveler can once again view prairiescapes filled with buffalo nurturing their newborn calves. From Arizona to Alaska, small herds still nibble buffalo grass in summer and wait out winter storms for the first buds of spring. In preserves such as South Dakota's Custer State Park, throngs of visitors, foreign and domestic, still can experience a bygone era—a time when the grasslands were darkened by massive herds of buffalo whose stampedes would make the ground rumble and the sod fly.

A heartier animal likely never roamed the range. With man's assistance, a more noble beast was never closer to vanishing from the face of the earth.

As civilization surrounds us with increasing intensity in each passing year, the saga of the American bison provides reassurance that man can care for more than himself—that a passionate commitment to preserving his fellow creatures may indeed be his most enduring legacy.

THE BUFFALO COOKBOOK

PREFACE

After my husband David's heart attack in the late eighties, I became compulsively conscious of what he ate. Fat and cholesterol were as closely monitored as his blood pressure and pulse. Equally concerned about our young son Jordan, who was tested and found to have hereditary high cholesterol, diet and nutrition became my primary focus. After many consultations with hospital dieticians and outside nutritionists, we were given charts, books, and the clear message, "No Red Meat!" As a good dietary student frightened by our situation, I diligently followed the dictates of the hospital, making the directives a learning process. We eliminated red meat from our diet and transformed all of the gourmet cooking my family had become accustomed to into healthy and acceptable "heart smart" cuisine.

Challenges always entice me...the bigger the challenge, the more interesting it becomes. We began eating endless quantities of vegetables, fruits, chicken, turkey, and tofu (higher in fat, but still legitimate). Still, we longed for that juicy burger or succulent rare steak.

Three years later and tofued into oblivion, David and I were in South Dakota, as David was commissioned to do the painting for Mt. Rushmore's fiftieth-anniversary celebration. Numerous local eateries were serving buffalo burgers and other bison specialties—touting this game as a healthy alternative to beef. The claims were accurate; there was virtually no fat present in the meat. Buffalo/bison became the salvation of our dietary dilemma!

THE BUFFALO COOKBOOK

INTRODUCTION

I have always had an enduring interest in fine food and cooking. My father's livelihood came from the food industry. During my early childhood he co-owned the EVERKRISP Potato Chip Company in Detroit, Michigan, and continued to work in that industry throughout his lifetime. His owning the company meant Saturday mornings filled with play and fantasy in the factory. I would ride the enormous three-sided potato chip carts as if they were spaceship scooters equipped with paste-on knobs and boxed snack foods for my departure. On other frequent visits, I would gleefully devour hot potato chips right off the conveyor belt—what a taste sensation, nothing like what one buys packaged off the shelves!

Throughout my childhood and young adult life, I was exposed to many types of foods as well as cuisine from many parts of the world. We ate in restaurants most of the time as my mother, who truly enjoyed eating fine food, had no interest in preparing it. Knowing and accepting her own limitations, the family joke became: Mom knows what and where to order out—"she *does* do reservations well." Perhaps some of this attitude came from her upbringing in what she considered a more sophisticated atmosphere, New York. Comfort food as we know it did not exist in our house. For me, learning how to cook was purely self-defense.

Flavor in the fifties meant fat and salt—any herbs or spices in our sparsely filled spice rack were used only when we were fortunate enough to have someone other than Mom cooking a holiday meal. Pilaf with its nutty flavor and spice-laden Dolmades were a special treat when our Armenian neighbors would graciously hand deliver a platter to our door.

During my college days, cooking became more than a necessity or a hobby. What came out of ironing fancy grilled cheese sandwiches on the ironing board in the dorm became monumental experimentation in an apartment, and classes were not purely of an academic nature. Ethnic-inspired foods were my specialty in those days...and still are (it must have been that wonderful early Armenian experience)!

Today I look at food differently: I consider fat, I regard herbs and spices, and I glory in the creation of new and exciting recipes that are not only deliciously flavorful, but healthy. Included in this book are recipes I have developed since our real introduction to bison/buffalo meat while in South Dakota. These recipes are tried, tested, and part of our family's daily dining as well as meals I prepare for friends and clients alike.

The recipes included here are all low fat and designed to keep you within a legitimate dietary framework. I make no claims to be a doctor, dietitian, or nutritionist—just a food writer sharing carefully researched information that I hope provides a new and exciting alternative for those who share our dietary dilemma.

Some of my recipes may seem labor intensive; do not be frightened off. Not every recipe is designed to be a quick and easy family dinner. The more laborious ones can be for those evenings set aside to invite special guests. As a working member of my family, there are many evenings I want to come home after a busy day of business meetings or writing sessions and prepare simple meals. On the other hand, spending several hours on a weekend afternoon "creating" a unique and delicious meal for friends is, for me, therapeutic—not an intimidation of palatal conquests. I approach cooking as I do life: as a delectable art form filled with adventure.

Many recipes in *The Buffalo Cookbook* utilize numerous and unusual herbs and spices. If you are lacking a full selection of pantry seasonings, substitute what you may already have...ground Kosher salt certainly does what sea salt does; exchanging herbs and spices may provide you with a different combination of diverse tastes. If you choose to closely follow my recipes, your outcome will be successful; if you choose to experiment, you will learn to create.

THE BUFFALO COOKBOOK

FACTS ABOUT BISON

Within recorded history, no species of large game has ever equalled the number of the American bison (*Bison bison)*. This, the largest member of the *Bovidae* family of mammals, includes cattle, goats, sheep, and oxen. The interchangeable name buffalo has questionable beginnings. The Spaniards identified them as "bulls," "wild cows," and "oxen." Some believe it came from the mispronunciation of the French word for beef, *boeuf.* Thus, the term bison and buffalo are used not correctly, but compatibly. Weighing 1,500 to 2,000 pounds, the mature bull can stand over six feet tall at the hump and can measure beyond nine feet from the muzzle to the tail. Female cows are smaller, weighing 900 to 1,200 pounds, ranging from about five feet tall at the hump and measuring over six feet from the muzzle to the tail.

The horns, hoofs, and muffle (bare part of the upper lip and nose) are primarily black in color. The most singular feature of this unpredictable bovine ruminant is the large shoulder hump which accounts for the appearance that the hindquarters are off perspective. There are no significant color changes between the sexes. Color gradation can occur from one herd to another or from one gene pool to another. The dark, wooly hair on the shoulders is longer and more shaggy than on other parts of the body. The life span of a bison is twenty to forty years; sexual maturation develops at age two.

These animals adapt to all surroundings and weather changes. In the dead of winter they will graze into the wind, foraging onward, patiently dealing with the numbing cold, drifting snow, and winter storms. The docile grazing posture of this mammal is deceptive. Bison are innate chargers with unreliable behavior; they should always be viewed with respect and trepidation. An agitated buffalo can wind or even outrun a fast horse.

HISTORY

OF THE AMERICAN BISON

Historic accounts by early European explorers document that Hernando Cortez was the first European to see an American bison at the palace of the great Aztec ruler, Montezuma. This bison was a captive in a menagerie and was approximately 300 miles south of the species' geographic range.

The Spanish explorer Alvar Nunez Cubeza de Vaca first sighted a few bison on their natural range in 1530. This new "cow" was a curiosity, but it was not until 1542 that there seemed to be an understanding that there were hundreds of thousands. It was then that Francisco Vasquez Coronado sighted great numbers of the shaggy beasts and sent word back to Spain of the enormity of numbers concerning the new cattle which appeared as a "brown sea." Pedro de Castaneda stated that there were so many cows in this country it was impossible to number them as they were "...as plentiful as the fish in the sea."

From written accounts, it is clear that buffalo outnumbered human inhabitants of North America and covered the eastern two-thirds of the continent.

SHARING THE LAND

Native Americans shared this land with the bison. It is estimated there were between 60 and 100 million buffalo roaming freely on the plains. With few natural enemies outside of man, prairie fires, and thin ice formations over deep water, it seemed the shaggy beasts would always remain.

For generations, the Plains Indians were dependant on these animals for their sustenance. Most Plains Indians were nomads. They followed the tremendous herds as the animals traveled with their calves across the great plains. The bison were more than just a food source for many Native Americans; they played a prominent role in influencing their way of life and all that was attached to it. Although the tribes differed, their utilizations and customs retained a similarity.

All parts of the buffalo were used by these indigenous people. The meat was eaten: raw, cooked, or dried. Some tribes actually preferred their meat rancid. The Mandans were so fond of putrid meat, they buried the bison whole during the winter and retrieved it in the spring for eating.

Loads of carcasses would be found at bends in rivers where the buffalo, misreading the snowy terrain, would find themselves on ice. Their massive weight would cause them to cave through the ice and drown in the cold, deep waters. The indigenous inhabitants would eat the meat from the carcasses regardless of how long they had been submerged and rotting.

A large bull could provide up to 900 pounds of edible meat; a cow, 500 pounds. The tongue, heart, brain, kidneys, liver, lungs, intestines, testicles, and sweetbreads were all eaten. The hump made a delicious roast; the blood was used in soups and puddings.

Buffalo delicacies differed among tribes. The Pawnee and the Cheyenne fancied roasted lungs. The Cheyenne baked fresh hides for consumption, over ground pits. The Cree relished udder fat. Other tribes grilled the entire udder, filled with milk, from a lactating buffalo cow. Some northern tribes favored a dish made from fetal buffalo calves. When Native Americans found themselves in enemy territory, they made entire meals out of raw buffalo. Knowing that fire and smoke would surely disclose their location, they made bowls from the buffalo ribs to prepare pudding made of brains and marrow, and ate the remaining organs as garnish, washing the meat down with blood. Few parts of the buffalo escaped the Indians' culinary curiosities or needs—many that would seem repugnant to non-Indian palates.

▲▲▲▲▲▲▲▲▲▲◇▲▲▲▲▲▲▲▲▲▲

COOKING AND STORING

General cooking methods varied. Meat was often broiled, stewed, smoked, roasted, and boiled. Buffalo meat was also commonly cooked by suspending a fresh buffalo paunch from four sticks, creating a sack, partially filling it with water, and adding heated stones to bring the water to a boil—then, strips of meat were added briefly to cook. This method was appropriately called stone boiling. Regardless of how meat was prepared, it was always preferred rare.

After a big hunt, it was common for the tribe to cache part of the meat. This form of storing varied among tribes—some buried the meat, others piled it under hides. In winter months, there were those who stored the meat in mounds of snow. Caching proved to be a temporary means of storage for the meat, while jerking (dehydrating) the meat would prevent it from spoiling for up to three years in the relative dryness of the West.

Pemmican was made and stored for times when fresh meat was not available. This process was the precursor of truly preserved foodstuffs, and enabled preservation up to thirty years. The technique of making pemmican varied from tribe to tribe; the difference generally being regional. The basic pemmican recipe consisted of abrading jerky and packing it into bags made of buffalo hide. Atop the jerky, hot marrow fat was poured to encase each and every morsel of meat; some tribes added berries and/or nuts. Each bag was stitched and then sealed with tallow along all seams. Prior to hardening, the rawhide bags were compressed into flat pillowcase-sized packages weighing approximately ninety pounds. This made the "pieces" (as they were called) more portable.

The northwesterner, David Thompson, stated that, "The best pemmican, was a mixture of fifty pounds of beat meat and twenty each of two kinds of fat, plus a goodly quantity of maple sugar or of dried berries as sweet as the best currants."

NATIVE AMERICAN GENDER ROLES

The job of butchering the meat fell into the category that included men as well as women, depending on the specific tribe. During this tedious process of butchering, slicing, and separating, those who butchered, sampled raw fragments as they worked.

The tribe women's duties were vast. The hides were predominantly handled by the women of the tribe. The dressed hides became multitudes of objects, clothing, and equipment: moccasins, leggings, dresses, breechclouts, belts, mittens, tobacco pouches, knife sheaths, lashings, shields, medicine cases, cooking vessels, drums, waterproof containers, saddle bags, boats, ceremonial rattles, masks, snowshoes, and sweathouse coverings. The most important and ingenious of these rawhide articles was the parfleche, a suitcase-type box that folded, and was used for travel

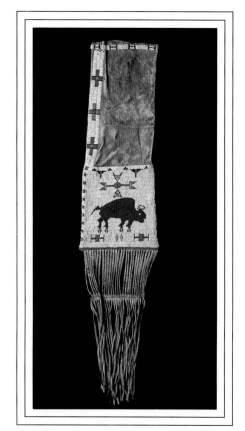

Tobacco bag. Tribe: Sioux, circa 1890.
Courtesy of Richard Pohrt and Dick Pohrt, Jr.
Photo: Tim Thayer

and storage. Robe-tanned hides were made into outer apparel and blankets as they were tanned with the hair remaining. Wet rawhide shrank as it dried thus performing the function of glue and nails. Rawhide that was cured by numerous heat treatments enabled the hardened leather to deaden even a bullet.

Hair removed from the hides was used as stuffing for balls and dolls, braided into ropes, and made into jewelry, ornaments, and brushes. Today's modern practice of hair extension found roots in certain tribes, whereby the men would use bison hair to extend their own.

Tendons (or sinews) from the neck and back made incredibly strong thread for use in connecting and joining hides, the production of bowstrings, and the wrapping of arrowheads.

Buffalo horn spoon. Tribe: Osage, circa 1860.
Courtesy of Richard Pohrt and Dick Pohrt, Jr.
Photo: Tim Thayer

Internal organs of the bison were used for a variety of carrying devices. The paunch, being the most versatile, was removed from the carcass, cleaned, dried, and utilized for water canteens and the storage of marrow and meat. The large intestine, the membranous sac which encased the heart, and the bladder were also used in the fashion of a paunch bag.

Buffalo bones were used in making hide scrapers, awls, knives, war clubs, runners for sleds, paint brush handles, ornaments, spades, hoes, game dice, counters for gambling games, toys, and jewelry.

Teeth of the buffalo fulfilled the purpose of ornamentation on clothing and accessories; generally only incisors from the bottom jaw were used (not molar teeth). Bison horns were transformed into ornamental designs for headdresses and masks, cups, spoons, ladles, implements for handling hot coals, and black powder flasks. The tails were utilized as fly swatters, knife sheath ornaments, and water whisks for the sweat houses. Back fat of the bison was used as hair grease as well as an ingredient for soap.

Buffalo dung was a valuable commodity to plains dwellers as buffalo chips were used as a fuel source. These chips are almost totally impermeable to wet weather conditions and produce a long-lasting, clean, hot fire for cooking and warmth.

▲▲▲▲▲▲▲▲▲▲◇▲▲▲▲▲▲▲▲▲▲

THE KILL

The hunt and kill for bison was a skill, a talent that was perfected long before Native Americans acquired horses or guns. Indian hunters could shoot arrows almost as quickly as white men could fire six shooters. Arrows revealed the identity of the slayer and thus, the rights to each slain buffalo. Each hunter could single out his own arrows.

The bows that accompanied the arrows were made from a variety of materials. Some bows were made of hardwood, Osage orange or cedar—others were made of buffalo horns and elk antlers. Bow strings were made from sinews. Arrow heads and lances were headed with stone (obsidian) or horn, and in later times, tipped with iron or steel on a base of dogwood or cane.

These able hunters used a variety of methods to kill bison. The "surround" meant just what it implies—a cordon was formed by a band of hunters on foot, slowly reducing the size of the circle around the frantic buffalo, and culminating in lance throwing or arrow shooting at close range.

"Impounding" was the method of driving the buffalo within a "pound" or a pen made of rock, piled brush, and/or wood that formed a corral and allowed for a contiguous kill.

The famous "pishkin" (piskun, pishkun) or "buffalo jump" began as stampedes by the tribesman to instigate running bison to jump over a cliff and either fall to their death or be badly maimed—then the crippled animal could easily be killed. These mass killings had to be planned for areas of rough terrain. "Fire drives" and the use of "runners" (young single males from the tribe disguised as decoys) were other means of inciting the huge animals to charge over a precipice.

Journal Entry of Merriweather Lewis, famed explorer:
Wednesday May 29th 1805

> *"Today we passed on the Stard. side the remains of a vast many mangled carcases of Buffalow which had been driven over a precipice of 120 feet by the Indians and perished; the water appeared to have washed away a part of this immence pile of slaughter and still their remained the fragments of at least a hundred carcases they created a most horrid stench. in this manner the Indians of the Missouri distroy vast herds of buffaloe at a stroke; for this purpose one of the most active and fleet young men is scelected and disguised in a robe of buffaloe skin, having also the skin of the buffaloe's head with the years and horns fastened on his head in form of a cap, thus caparisoned he places himself at a convenient distance between a herd of buffaloe and a precipice proper for the purpose, which happens in many places on this river for miles together; the other indians now surround the herd on the back and flanks and at a signal agreed on all shew themselves at the same time moving forward towards the buffaloe; the disguised indian or decoy has taken care to place himself sufficiently nigh the buffaloe to be noticed by them when they take to flight and runing before them they follow him in full speede*

*to the precipice, the cattle behind driving those in front over
and seeing them go do not look or hesitate about following
untill the whole are precipitated down the precipice forming
one common mass of dead an[d] mangled carcases: the decoy in the mean time has taken care to secure himself in some
cranney or crivice of the clift which he had previously prepared for that purpose. the part of the decoy I am informed is
extreamly dangerous, if they are not very fleet runners the buffaloe tread them under foot and crush them to death, and
sometimes drive them over the precipice also, where they per-
ish in common with the buffaloe..."*

The high drama of the buffalo jumps were frequently depicted graphically in paint-
ings of that time. In Montana alone, there are hundreds of jumps recorded. Many

pishkin sites still exist and have been the locations of numerous archaeological
findings.

The term "still hunting" was literal; this required the hunter to disguise his scent
and hide in a place the buffalo would frequent. This method of killing was made
easier if the bison was caught in a bog, trapped by thin ice, or crippled by a fall.
The "running hunt" became effective in the sixteenth century, once the Native
Americans acquired horses from the Spaniards. Mounted, the hunters could ride
into the herd and shoot arrows into the buffalo at proximate range.

For hundreds of years, Native Americans killed for their needs without unneces-
sary depletion and with undeniable respect for the great herds.

"The buffaloes were more frequent that I have ever seen cattle in the settlements,
browsing on the leaves of cane, or cropping the herbage of those extensive plains,
fearless because ignorant of man. Sometimes we saw hundreds in a drove, and the
numbers about the salt spring were amazing," reports Daniel Boone in 1770. Igno-
rance of man did not spare these great shaggy creatures.

Due to the impenetrable foliage over the entire Atlantic Slope, buffalo herds num-
bered far less than the immense herds of the treeless plains where they were
counted by continual days when they were not lost sight of, rather than in actual
numbers.

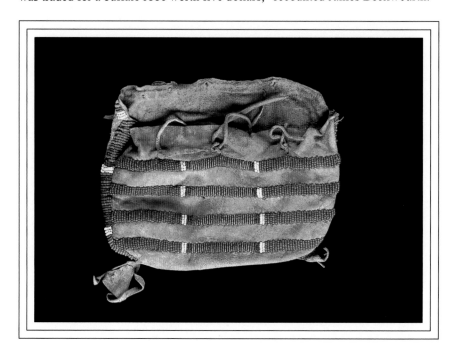

THE ROLE OF THE FRONTIERSMEN

Fur trading had its beginnings in the late 1600s. Tribesmen on the plains became prosperous, which soon altered aspects of their tribal customs and their relationship to the buffalo. Bartering power, along with firearms, established the perception of personal property. Fur traders utilizing the barter concept and instilling the taste of acquisitions directed the Native Americans into unfair trades.

"Four gallons of water were added to each gallon of alcohol, and a pint of the stuff was traded for a buffalo robe worth five dollars," recounted James Beckwourth.

Storage bag. Tribe: Crow, circa 1870.
Courtesy of Richard Pohrt and Dick Pohrt, Jr.
Photo: Tim Thayer

The early 1800s brought Merriweather Lewis and William Clark, to open the northwest, which furthered the demands for buffalo robes. This point in time also marked an interest in buffalo as a food source and a delicacy for the frontiersman.

"My fare is really sumptuous this evening; buffaloe's humps, tongues and marrow bones, fine trout parched meal pepper and salt, and a good appetite; the last is not considered the least of the Luxuries," related in the journals of Lewis and Clark (dated Thursday, June 13, 1805).

Frontier gourmets believed the tongue was the greatest delicacy. Some relished roasted ribs and marrow. "Hunter's Butter" or "Prairie Butter" were terms attached to the marrow that was used as a spread for biscuits. Others believed the hump was the most exceptional part of the bison.

"...equal to any meat I ever saw, and we feasted sumptuously on the choice morsels," Zebulon Montgomery Pike recorded about buffalo meat in his journals of 1806.

By converting a typical army wagon, Charles Goodnight developed the "chuck wagon" in the 1850s. Goodnight, the frontiersman, wanted his meat to be buffalo

Buffalo grazing.
Courtesy of South Dakota Department of Tourism

which he "considered a necessity for longevity." It is further documented that he had a small personal herd to make the finest elixir ever devised—a mixture of buffalo meat and hard whiskey.

The established need and dependence by frontiersmen upon buffalo incorporated far more than first realized by these adventurers. Travelers in need of drink quenched their thirst with the contents of the animals paunch. This gelatinous green juice saved many lives on the expansive plains.

As the white man continued to invade the plains, the bison continued to be ravaged for their tongues and hides. The tongues and robes became big business and the mere killing of the great beasts became sport for white hunters.

From the journals of Maximillian dated June 24, 1833:

"In a recent year, the fur company sent 42,000 of these hides down the river, which were sold, in the United States, at four dollars a-piece. Fort Union alone consumes about 600 to 800 buffaloes annually, and the other forts in proportion. The numerous Indian tribes subsist almost entirely on these animals, sell their skins after retaining a sufficient supply for their clothing, tents, &c., and the agents of the Company recklessly shoot down these noble animals for their own pleasure, often not making the least use of them, except taking out the tongue. While herds of them are often drowned in the Missouri; nay, I have been assured that, in some rivers, 1,800 and more of their dead bodies were found in one place. Complete dams are formed of the bodies of these animals in some of the morasses of the rivers; from this we may form some idea of the decrease of the buffaloes, which are now found on the other side of the Rocky Mountains, where they were not originally met with, but whither they have been driven."

▲▲▲▲▲▲▲▲▲▲◆▲▲▲▲▲▲▲▲▲▲

THE EXPANSION OF THE RAILROADS

The slaughter manifested as never before as 1860 brought the building of the railroads. To eliminate their roadblocks and to feed their crews, hired guns were employed by the railroad managers. William F. Cody signed on as a hunter for the Kansas Pacific Railroad in 1867. In one year, Cody single-handedly killed 4,000 buffalo to feed the track-laying crew and was given the nickname "Buffalo Bill."

With the lines in place and the increase of railway companies, buffalo hunting became entertainment and the demise of the buffalo became a reality. Within a seventy-year time frame, beginning around 1800, millions of bison had been annihilated. Distress over their meat supply caused the Indians to attack the whites on the Great Plains.

As the herds dwindled, tribes began to loose their nomadic lifestyle and independence. Too late to change the outcome, the starving tribes people were forced to accept removal from their homeland and placement on regulated federal reservations.

The Union Pacific Railroad reached Cheyenne, Wyoming, in 1867. This railway's east-west lines divided the plains buffalo into a northern and southern herd. The end of the great southern herd came in 1875. Seven million pounds of buffalo bones and 200,000 hides were auctioned off in Fort Worth, Texas.

▲▲▲▲▲▲▲▲▲▲◆▲▲▲▲▲▲▲▲▲▲

U.S. GOVERNMENT INVOLVEMENT

A Congressional Bill was passed by the House and Senate to stop the unconscionable slaughter of the bison; President Grant refused to sign the bill. Then Secretary of the Interior, Columbus Delano was quoted as saying he would rejoice when the last bison was exterminated.

The government's policy on hunting buffalo was reflected in General Phillip Sheridans's speech:

"These men have done in the last two years and will do in the next year, more to settle the vexed Indian question than the entire regular army has done in the last thirty years. They are destroying the Indians's commissary, and it is a well known fact that an army losing its base of supplies is placed at a great disadvantage. Send them powder and lead, if you will; but, for the sake of lasting peace, let them kill, skin, and sell until the buffaloes are exterminated. Then your prairies can be covered with speckled cattle and the festive cowboy, who follows the hunter as a second forerunner of an advanced civilization."

There was no direct order given to the army to obliterate the remaining bison, just free ammunition making it perfectly clear.

THE PAST AND THE FUTURE

Treaties and promises broken, herds disappearing, prairiescapes white with skeletons of the great beasts, bones shipped by the tons for fertilizer and bone china—nothing remained of the past.

The end of the great northern herd came in 1883, and by the turn of the century, there were less than 1,000 remaining bison.

Zoologist William Temple Hornaday wrote *The Extermination of the American Bison* which was published by the United States Government in 1888. Rather late in the course of events, the purpose of this publication was to instill public awareness and fuel concern over the imminent extinction of the buffalo. In May of 1894, Congress finally passed a law, signed by President Grover Cleveland, to protect the species from extinction.

The last remaining bison in the United States could be found in small privately owned herds and a few government controlled preserves, such as Yellowstone National Park.

Efforts by conservationists and sympathetic politicians—Hornaday, Ernest Harold Baynes, Martin Garretson, George Bird Grinell, and President Theodore Roosevelt—finally brought the message to the American public. On December 8, 1905, the American Bison Society was established. Its elected officers reflected the commitment necessary to change public opinion and convince Congress to form Conservational Refuges for the bison.

Within a ten-year period, the Wichita Game Preserve in Oklahoma, the Flathead Indian Reservation in Montana, the Niobrara National Wildlife Refuge in Nebraska, Wind Cave National Park, and Custer State Park in South Dakota were organized and allocated initial buffalo stock from private herds, some by purchase and some by donation.

Almost one century later, the bison are returning to the plains—herds jointly totaling over 150,000 head are sprinkled throughout the United States on private ranches, national parks, and government sanctuaries. No longer on the brink of extinction, these noble beasts remain a significant part of our history—intertwined with our past and ecologically connected to our present.

"The ground on which we stand is sacred ground. It is the dust and blood of our ancestors. On these plains the Great White Father in Washington sent his soldiers armed with long knives and rifles to slay the Indian. Many of them sleep on yonder hill where Pahaska—White Chief of the Long Hair [General Custer]—so bravely fought and fell.

"A few more passing suns will see us here no more, and our dust and bones will mingle with these same prairies. I see as in a vision the dying spark of our council fires, the ashes cold and white. I see no longer the curling smoke rising from our lodge poles. I hear no longer the songs of the women as they prepare the meal.

"The antelope have gone; the buffalo wallows are empty. Only the wail of the coyote is heard. The white man's medicine is stronger than ours; his iron horse [the railroad] rushes over the buffalo trail. He talks to us through his "whispering spirit" [the telephone].

"We are like birds with a broken wing. My heart is cold within me. My eyes are growing dim—I am old."

*Chief Plenty Coups
Crow (1849-1932)*

FACTS

ABOUT BISON MEAT

Crow parfleche buffalo rawhide, circa 1850.
The Chandler-Pohrt Collection,
Courtesy of the Detroit Institute of Arts

The appearance of raw bison meat displays a deep red-brown hue, rich in color. Specific cuts of meat appear similar to that of beef, although bison contains virtually no marbling (naturally produced internal streaks of fat). This intense blood red color is due in part to the lack of marbling as well as the high iron content. Factors that cause a variance in meat color are: age, feeding, storage, handling, and food processing.

Bison are not given hormones, low-level antibiotics, nitrites, or preservatives, deeming them at this date an allergy-free meat.

Presently, bison are not covered by the Mandatory Federal Meat Inspection Act and does not have to be USDA approved. A voluntary inspection program has been established, and it is the option of the meat producer to utilize that program. Retail outlets selling bison meat generally demand inspection regardless of the standards. Most U.S. producers utilize the inspection process.

The beef industry maintains a grading system to establish relative meat quality. The guidelines provided encompass primarily marbling and age of the animal at time of slaughter. Due to the public emphasis on "lean" meat, it is a difficult and outdated system to maintain. This federal grading scale does not apply to bison meat.

The most lean cut of any meat will always come from whole, single muscles, leaving no seam fat (the layer between individual muscles).

The tenderloin and rib eye are the most tender area. The rib eye is boneless and can be used in any recipe calling for filets or tournedos. A rib steak, which is also very tender, does have the bone attached.

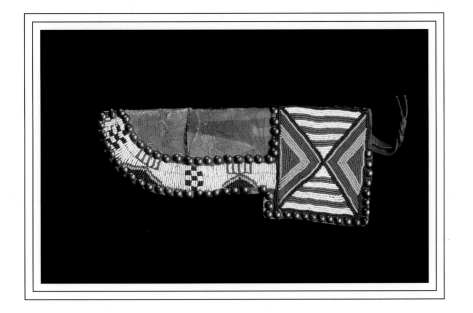

Knife case. Tribe: Assinaboin, circa 1870.
Courtesy of Richard Pohrt and Dick Pohrt, Jr.
Photo: Tim Thayer

▲▲▲▲▲▲▲▲▲▲◆▲▲▲▲▲▲▲▲▲▲

BUFFALO CUTS

1. ROUND—rump roast, top round roast, bottom round roast **2. SIRLOIN**—steak, short loin–tenderloin roast, porterhouse steak, T-bone steak, filet mignon, medallions **3. RIB**—rib eye roast, rib eye steak, ribs **4. CHUCK**—chuck eye roast, stew meat, ground meat **5. CHUCK**—round bone roast, ground meat **6. FLANK**—flank steak, ground meat, stew meat, brisket **7. ROUND**—round steak, roast, ground meat

The top loin section would include a variety of steak and roast cuts all coming from the short loin (T-bone, porterhouse, and strip steak).

Bison should be slaughtered (processed) between the ages of eighteen months and two-and-a-half years. As with other meats, age plays a major factor in the tenderness of the meat.

The taste of bison need not be an acquired one; there is no "gamey" quality only a subtle sweetness and a closely related taste to that of the traditional red meat, beef. Bison meat will differ slightly in taste depending on where the bison was raised and ranged and if it has been custom fed with a grain base.

With its obvious similarities to beef, bison can be substituted in all recipes requiring red meat; but it must be cooked differently.

Due to the lack of natural fat in bison meat, it is essential that this meat not be overcooked to retain its natural tenderization.

Bison needs to be cooked slow, low, and not as thoroughly as beef (specifically rare to medium). With the fat content of bison being so low, this meat can be eaten rare with no concern over additional fat content. Other meats, if eaten rare, will contain a higher fat content than those well cooked.

The density of this meat provides a more satisfying portion, allowing for a reduction in quantity per person.

Lone buffalo.
Courtesy of the
South Dakota Department of Tourism

32
FACTS ABOUT
BISON MEAT

My kitchen.
Photo: Jim Hedrich
©Hedrich-Blessing
permission of
Country Home Magazine

▲▲▲▲▲▲▲▲▲▲▲▲▲▲▲▲▲▲▲▲▲▲▲▲▲▲▲▲▲▲▲

GENERAL DIRECTIONS

FOR COOKING BISON

▼▼▼▼▼▼▼▼▼▼▼▼▼▼▼▼▼▼▼▼▼▼▼▼▼▼▼▼▼

Bison meat is naturally tender. If cooked improperly the meat will become tough, dry, and unpalatable.

Meat should be cooked slowly at low to medium temperatures. Bison meat cooks faster than beef. As there is no fat to act as an insulator to the meat, the meat is cooked directly.

Recommended cooking range is rare to medium and internal temperatures should be 135 degrees–155 degrees Farenheit. The FDA has set cooking guidelines to 155 degrees for restaurants, insuring the safety of bacterial concerns.

▲▲▲▲▲▲▲▲▲◆▲▲▲▲▲▲▲▲▲

ROASTS

When preparing a roast, preheat the oven to 275–325 degrees. Let the roast come to room temperature prior to cooking. When ready, cook consistently at one temperature throughout the cooking process. Use a meat thermometer to keep an accurate register of internal temperature, inserting the pointed end of the meat thermometer into the thickest portion of the roast. If the roast is not deboned, make sure the thermometer is placed in the meat with no interference. Instant read thermometers are an alternative to the standard meat thermometer; this thermometer is not to be left in the meat during the cooking process. An instant read is a quick response thermometer which probes the meat and provides you with the internal temperature.

Less tender cuts of meat require liquid or marinade to aid in the cooking process, i.e. chuck, hump, and round roasts. Acidic liquids and marinades also aid in tenderization. Browning all sides of the roast will also help with retention of moisture. The usual cooking rules do not apply with these cuts; they need to be cooked longer—until the meat becomes tender.

Tenderloin, rib eye, and top round roasts require no liquids or sauces, although they may be used. These roasts should only be cooked from rare to medium-rare range.

There are numerous methods of cooking bison roasts; it truly becomes a matter of preference. Options include: slow cookers, plastic cooking bags, foil-wrapped low roasters, dutch ovens, brown bags, and uncovered low pans suitable for oven use.

STEAKS

Bison steaks come in a wide variety of cuts, all comparable with beef. Most butchers and/or meat producers will cut steaks to customer specifications (1 inch to 1-1/4 inch are preferred).

Methods of cooking steaks include: grilling (outdoor or on top of stove), pan sauteing, broiling, and stir frying. Do not overcook; readjust thinking as well as the heat source.

Grilling time will vary depending on the temperature of the coals and whether the meat is placed on or off the rack. An instant read thermometer comes in handy for outdoor grilling.

Steaks do not need additional liquid, sauces, or marinades unless desired. Frequent turning of the meat is recommended.

GROUND MEAT

Ground bison meat comes from a variety of cuts: trimming from steaks, chuck, rib section, hump, shank, and less tender roast areas.

This lean ground meat is delicious simply as a burger or made into a variety of diverse recipes. Ground bison can be incorporated into a multitude of familiar dishes. Methods of cooking ground bison include: grilling (outdoor or on top of stove), broiling, and pan sautéing (covered or uncovered). Keep in mind that bison meat cooks faster and remains the same size throughout cooking.

As with all other types of bison meat, cook this meat low, slow, and lightly browned.

HANDLING AND STORAGE OF BISON MEAT

As with any meat, make sure your hands are washed and clean before handling (as well as any equipment that is to be used in the cooking process).

Storage of fresh bison meat is best in the coldest section of the refrigerator. Some refrigerators have the capability to change coldness settings; if there is a great deal

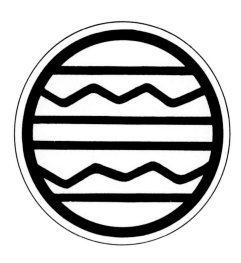

34
GENERAL DIRECTIONS
FOR COOKING BISON

of meat to store, you may want to select that option. Ground bison should not remain uncooked for more than a couple of days; roasts and steaks, no longer than four days. In any case, the meat should be in unopened packages and used as quickly as possible to retain freshness.

Producers freeze bison meat at -10 degrees F. to -30 degrees F. for preservational purposes. When meat is quick frozen, it allows for the smallest amount of crystalization and extinguishes or arrests potential organisms that produce spoilage. The meat is then stored at 0 degrees Fahrenheit; and if kept frozen, the meat will retain its freshness for a good six- to nine-month period.

To defrost bison meat, the United States Department of Agriculture (USDA) recommends placing it in the refrigerator for twenty-four hours to defrost slowly. Microwaves have the capability to defrost—a note of warning—if not carefully monitored, parts of the meat will actually begin to cook and appear brown in color. Meat can be cooked from the frozen stage—again a note of warning—this process must be closely monitored and internal temperature checked. Once the meat is pliable, insert a meat thermometer or cut (to be visually judged).

Like all other meats, do not re-freeze once defrosted.

ALL OF THE FOODS PHOTOGRAPHED IN THIS BOOK ARE FULLY COOKED AND PREPARED AS DIRECTED IN THE RECIPES. THERE IS NO ADDITIONAL RETOUCHING OF THE PHOTOGRAPHS WHATSOEVER.

COOK'S NOTES

"Casserole" in the following recipes is used interchangeably with a "Dutch oven," "French oven," or various size pots; they may be glass, enamel, porcelain, or cast-iron cookware with tight-fitting covers which will be specified when used.

GROUND MEAT

RECIPES

INGREDIENTS

FOR THE POTATO CRUST

	No-stick cooking spray
1	bulb garlic
2	pounds red-skin potatoes
¼	cup skim milk
	Dash of sea salt
	Dried parsley (for top garnish)

FOR THE FILLING

1	pound ground bison/buffalo meat
1	large onion, peeled and diced
½	Scotch bonnet pepper, seeds removed and diced (wear rubber gloves!)
1	tablespoon *jerk seasoning (*for recipe)
½	teaspoon dried tarragon
	Black pepper, freshly ground
2–3	large fresh mushrooms, thinly sliced

---

* See Ingredient Index

Red-skin potatoes and garlic form a delicious top and bottom "crust." The spicy meat and mushroom layers complete this "meal-in-itself" casserole. A glass of bold red wine and steamed or braised green vegetables complete the meal.   Yield: 4 servings

DIRECTIONS

Spray any small ovenproof dish with no-stick cooking spray. Lightly spray the garlic bulb and place it on dish. Bake at 400 degrees for 30 minutes or until lightly browned and the garlic cloves are soft. Remove softened cloves and set aside to cool slightly.

Boil unpeeled potatoes until tender (approximately 20 minutes). Drain the potatoes, add the garlic and milk; mash (do not use a food processor to mash potatoes—it makes them too mushy). Add salt to taste.

While the potatoes are boiling, cook the meat. Lightly spray a skillet with no-stick cooking spray. Sauté the onion and Scotch bonnet pepper until tender. Add the ground meat and brown. Add the jerk seasoning, tarragon, and black pepper. Remove any excess liquid with baster and discard.

Lightly spray an ovenproof casserole serving dish with no-stick cooking spray. Place half of the mashed potato mixture in the casserole. Layer sliced mushrooms over the potatoes; add the meat mixture. Cover the meat with the remaining mashed potatoes and sprinkle with dried parsley. Bake at 350 degrees for 30 minutes or until well browned. Let it sit for 5–10 minutes before serving.

CALORIC CHART

380 Calories per Serving:	
30.549 g Protein	
59.083 g Carbohydrate	
2.498 g Total Fat:	0.886 g Saturated
	0.848 g Monounsaturated
	0.358 g Polyunsaturated
70.688 mg Cholesterol	
288.000 mg Sodium	
4.427 mg Iron	

BUFFALO BURGERS WITH SALSA

Take your typical burger, subtract much of the fat and add a spicy salsa and you have these sizzling buffalo burgers. Serve them on a hot summer's night right off the grill with a cool and tangy slaw and a big ear of corn.

Yield: 6–8 servings

DIRECTIONS

FOR THE SALSA

In a large mixing bowl, add the tomatoes, chilies, onion, sugar, salt and pepper. Set aside for approximately 1 hour to allow flavors to blend.

Chop the cilantro and add to the mixture. Chill.

FOR THE BUFFALO BURGERS

Grill the buffalo burgers on an outdoor or indoor grill. Remove from the heat and top with the salsa. The burgers may be served with or without a bun.

Serve additional salsa with corn chips as a side dish.

CALORIC CHART

```
                     297 Calories per Serving:
        37.464 g Protein
        27.895 g Carbohydrate
         3.643 g Total Fat:
                              0.986 g Saturated
                              1.027 g Monounsaturated
                              0.280 g Polyunsaturated

        88.047 mg Cholesterol
       776.000 mg Sodium
         4.905 mg Iron
```

INGREDIENTS

FOR THE SALSA

2 (28-ounce) cans seasoned diced *tomatoes

2–4 fresh green chilies, (mild, medium, or hot depending on your taste), stem removed, chilies seeded and diced

1 large onion, peeled and finely diced

1 tablespoon sugar
Sea salt
Black pepper, freshly ground

2 tablespoons chopped fresh cilantro, stems removed

FOR THE BUFFALO BURGERS

2–2½ pounds ground bison/buffalo meat each patty should be ⅓ of a pound in weight prior to cooking (the meat does not shrink)

6–8 light (low-fat) burger buns

---

* See Ingredient Index

BISON BREAD PIE
WITH SPICY TOMATO CHUTNEY

▲▲▲▲▲▲▲▲▲▲◆▲▲▲▲▲▲▲▲▲▲

This chutney would be good alone or on almost anything! I like to serve these meaty "half-moons" as appetizers, but make them a little larger and they're wonderful as entrees. They're completely enclosed, so pack them along on a picnic or in a lunch box.

Yield: 4 dozen pies and 2 cups of chutney (Serves 8)

INGREDIENTS

FOR THE BREAD DOUGH
4	cups all purpose flour
4	egg whites
2	tablespoons canola oil
1/4	cup *Laban (heavy strained yogurt)
2 1/2	teaspoons fast rise *yeast, 1/2 cup warm water *plus* 1 teaspoon sugar (place in glass bowl and cover with plastic wrap, let sit for 5 minutes)
1/8	cup water

FOR THE MEAT FILLING
1/2	cup pine nuts
1 1/2	tablespoons canola oil
1	medium Spanish onion, peeled and diced
4	garlic cloves, peeled and minced
1 1/2	pounds ground bison/buffalo meat
1/2	cup chopped flat parsley
1	teaspoon ground coriander seed
1	teaspoon *Syrian allspice (*for recipe)
1/8	teaspoon cayenne (or *Mombassa)
1	teaspoon ground cinnamon
	Sea salt
	No-stick cooking spray

*See Ingredient Index

DIRECTIONS

▲▲▲▲▲▲▲▲

FOR MAKING THE BREAD DOUGH

Place the flour, egg whites, oil, Laban, and yeast mixture in a food processor bowl and process with the steel S blade until the dough forms a ball on top of the blade.

Set the ball of dough in a glass bowl and cover it with plastic wrap. Place in a warm place for 1 hour or until the ball doubles in size.

FOR COOKING THE MEAT

Heat a dry skillet. Add the pine nuts and brown lightly. Remove nuts from the skillet and set aside.

Heat the oil in a skillet, sauté the onions and garlic until transparent. Add the meat and brown. Remove any excess liquid and discard. Add the parsley leaves, pine nuts, coriander seed, Syrian allspice, cayenne, cinnamon, and salt (to taste). Heat thoroughly. Set aside to cool.

FOR PUTTING THE BREAD PIES TOGETHER

When the dough has doubled and the meat has cooled (keep dough covered in plastic wrap), break off walnut-sized balls of dough. On a wooden board, flatten each ball and form into a circle with a rolling pin.

Place approximately 1/2 tablespoon of filling in lower half of circle (do not let the meat touch the edges of the dough). Fold the dough over filling and pinch the edges together to form a "crescent moon" shape.

Place the bread pies on a baking sheet sprayed with no-stick cooking spray. Bake for 30 minutes or until lightly browned.

Continued on page 42

INGREDIENTS
(CONTINUED)

FOR THE TOMATO CHUTNEY

½	cup white wine (tarragon) vinegar
½	cup white vinegar
1	medium Spanish onion, peeled and cut into ¾-inch cubes
3	garlic cloves, peeled and minced
1	tablespoon fresh ginger root, peeled and minced
½	cup firmly packed, light brown sugar
½	cup sugar
1	Scotch bonnet pepper, stem removed, seeded and minced (wear rubber gloves —very hot!)
1	cinnamon stick
1	tablespoon whole mustard seeds
1	teaspoon ground cardamom
½	teaspoon ground cloves
1	tablespoon *orange blossom water
1	(28-ounce) can seasoned diced *tomatoes, drained

*See Ingredient Index

DIRECTIONS
(CONTINUED)

FOR THE TOMATO CHUTNEY

In a medium saucepan, bring the wine vinegar, white vinegar, onion, garlic, ginger, brown sugar, granulated sugar, Scotch bonnet pepper, cinnamon stick, mustard seeds, cardamom, cloves, and orange blossom water to a boil. Reduce the heat, stir frequently, and simmer uncovered for 45–60 minutes (until thick).

Add the drained tomatoes. Bring mixture back to a boil and remove from the heat. Serve cool or at room temperature with the bread pies.

CALORIC CHART

599 Calories per Serving:

31.325 g Protein
91.379 g Carbohydrate
13.323 g Total Fat:

    1.922 g Saturated
    6.403 g Monounsaturated
    4.200 g Polyunsaturated

53.266 mg Cholesterol
401.000 mg Sodium
8.459 mg Iron

CURRIED EGGPLANT AND BUFFALO OVER BOW-TIE NOODLES

Eggplant fans will be in heaven with this quick and easy recipe. Serve to company as a first course or as part of a festive buffet. I like to serve a fresh spinach salad and fresh fruit with this Tuscan-inspired pasta dish.

Yield: 6–8 servings

DIRECTIONS

In a large pot fitted with a stainless-steel steamer, steam the eggplant until it is tender, approximately 20 minutes. Drain the eggplant and set aside.

Heat the oil in a large pot over medium-high heat. Add the onions and garlic and sauté until lightly browned. Turn the heat down to medium-low, add the ground meat and continue to cook until the meat is browned. Discard remaining liquid.

Add the steamed eggplant to the meat mixture and mix gently with a spatula (keeping eggplant from breaking). Add the tomato sauce and curry powder. Lightly mix. Adjust the seasonings.

Serve over cooked noodles.

CALORIC CHART

433 Calories per Serving:

35.076 g Protein
54.803 g Carbohydrate
7.413 g Total Fat:

1.694 g Saturated
1.534 g Monounsaturated
0.947 g Polyunsaturated

124.000 mg Cholesterol
415.000 mg Sodium
6.161 mg Iron

INGREDIENTS

1½ tablespoons light olive oil
4   onions, peeled and chopped into ¾-inch pieces
3   garlic cloves, peeled and minced
2   pounds ground bison/buffalo meat
2   medium eggplant, peeled and cut into 1-inch cubes
3   cups tomato sauce
4   teaspoons curry powder
    Sea salt
1   pound bow-tie noodles (or any other interesting shape, cooked according to package directions)

VEGETABLE-BISON
STUFFED GRAPE LEAVES

The filling takes just minutes to assemble...the work is in the rolling of these meat and rice sensations. It's easy to double the recipe to make a larger batch...they freeze beautifully for up to one month.   Yield: 10–12 servings

DIRECTIONS

In a large skillet, heat the oil over medium-high heat. Add the onions and minced garlic and sauté until lightly browned. Add the diced carrots and sauté for 7 more minutes. Add the diced cabbage and cook for 5 minutes longer. Add the mushrooms and continue to sauté for another 5 minutes.

In a very large bowl, mix the cooked vegetables, raw bison, and washed, raw brown rice. To that mixture add the tomatoes, tomato paste, mint, Syrian allspice, salt (to taste), cumin, cardamom, and black pepper. Mix well.

If using jarred grape leaves rinse them thoroughly. If using fresh grape leaves, blanch them in boiling water for two minutes (to wilt) and rinse immediately in cool water for easy handling. Place the leaves with the stems and veins facing up. Cut the stems off. Place one tablespoon (or more) of the meat mixture onto the lower center of the leaf (use your judgement as to how much to put in each leaf). Pull the leaf bottom over the mixture and roll gently, folding the sides over as you go (do not roll too tightly or too loosely—they should appear firm and neatly rolled).

Lightly spray no-stick cooking spray in a Dutch oven, copper bottom pot, casserole, or a large fish poacher. Line pot(s) with extra unfilled grape leaves. If using a fish poacher, you may want to also line it with slices of raw onion to protect the rolled leaves from burning. Arrange the stuffed leaves in the bottom of your cooking pan. Alternate direction of layers. Pour the lemon juice, water, and olive oil mixture over the layered, stuffed grape leaves.

Bring to a boil, reduce the heat, and simmer for 1 ½ plus hours until the leaves are cooked and the water is almost evaporated. Carefully check one grape leaf to make sure the rice is tender (remember, brown rice does not have the same texture as white rice and takes longer to cook).

Serve hot, cold, or at room temperature, with or without yogurt sauce. See the recipe for bison-pita sandwiches with yogurt sauce.

INGREDIENTS

1	tablespoon light olive oil
1	large Spanish onion, peeled and chopped
4	garlic cloves, peeled and minced
4	large carrots, ends cut, peeled and diced
¼	head of savoy cabbage, core removed and cabbage finely diced
6	large firm white mushrooms, diced
2	pounds ground bison/buffalo meat
2	cups natural brown rice
1	(28-ounce) can seasoned diced *tomatoes, drained
1	cup tomato paste
2¼	tablespoons dried mint
½	tablespoon *Syrian allspice (*for recipe)
½	tablespoon sea salt (optional)
½	tablespoon ground cumin
1	teaspoon ground cardamom
¼	teaspoon freshly ground black pepper
1–2	jars grape leaves or fresh leaves (60–75 plus) No-stick cooking spray Raw onion, sliced (optional)
1	cup lemon juice, *plus* ¼ cup water, *plus* 1 tablespoon olive oil (mixed together for steaming stuffed leaves)

---
* See Ingredient Index

CALORIC CHART

```
            312 Calories per Serving:
22.984 g Protein
45.266 g Carbohydrate
 5.463 g Total Fat:    1.058 g Saturated
                       2.567 g Monounsaturated
                       0.771 g Polyunsaturated
46.959 mg Cholesterol
403.000 mg Sodium
  6.292 mg Iron
```

Opposite page:
Photo: Fred Ferris

JORDAN'S FAVORITE MEATLOAF

INGREDIENTS

▲▲▲▲▲▲▲▲▲

3	medium onions, peeled and chopped
3	garlic cloves, peeled and minced
3	pounds ground bison/buffalo meat
2½	cups herbed seasoned stuffing mix, processed to fine bread crumbs
5	egg whites
¾	cup tomato juice
1	tablespoon lime juice
1	teaspoon dried basil
1	teaspoon dried oregano
2½	teaspoon sea salt
1	teaspoon cayenne (or *Mombassa)
½	teaspoon *Syrian allspice (*for recipe)
	No-stick cooking spray

*See Ingredient Index

When my son Jordan asked me to make his favorite dish I gladly complied and developed this tasty buffalo meatloaf that's simply wonderful. I like to serve this the old-fashioned way with fluffy mashed potatoes and crisp corn. (Makes great leftover sandwiches.) Cook either in an oven-proof casserole or two meatloaf pans.   Yield: 8–10 servings

DIRECTIONS

▲▲▲▲▲▲▲▲

Preheat the oven to 300 degrees.

In a large bowl, add the onions, garlic, ground meat, fine bread crumbs, egg whites, tomato juice, lime juice, basil, oregano, salt, cayenne, and Syrian allspice and mix thoroughly. Spray a 2½-quart ovenproof casserole serving dish with cooking spray.

Add the meat loaf mixture and bake for 1½ hours at 300 degrees or until nicely browned. Remove any excess liquid with a baster or carefully tilt to release any of the liquid.

Serve hot with mashed or baked potatoes and steamed vegetables.

CALORIC CHART

▲▲▲▲▲▲▲▲▲

232 Calories per Serving:	
33.262 g Protein	
15.810 g Carbohydrate	
3.130 g Total Fat:	0.964 g Saturated
	0.996 g Monounsaturated
	0.305 g Polyunsaturated
84.525 mg Cholesterol	
976.000 mg Sodium	
4.444 mg Iron	

SPAGHETTI WITH OPAL BASIL SAUCE

Nothing goes better with pasta than fresh basil. Opal basil has a distinct, intense taste. However, any variety of basil may be utilized with equal success. Use an unflavored pasta for best results; you'll allow the buffalo and basil flavors to dominate. For a complete change of pace, serve the sauce over brown or wild rice.   Yield: 12 servings

DIRECTIONS

FOR THE SAUCE

Heat the oil in a large casserole over medium-high heat. Add the onions and garlic and sauté until they appear transparent.

Add the bison meat and cook over medium-low heat until lightly browned. Discard any excess liquid.

Add the tomatoes and mix thoroughly. Add the opal basil, chili pepper flakes, Syrian allspice, and oregano. Simmer for 5 minutes, stirring frequently.

Add the tomato sauce and tomato paste. Continue to cook over medium-low heat for an additional 45 minutes.

Adjust all seasonings to taste.

Continue to cook for an additional 20 minutes. Serve over cooked pasta.

CALORIC CHART

565 Calories per Serving:	
42.867 g Protein	
82.336 g Carbohydrate	
6.352 g Total Fat:	1.475 g Saturated
	1.146 g Monounsaturated
	0.886 g Polyunsaturated
82.178 mg Cholesterol	
921.000 mg Sodium	
8.454 mg Iron	

INGREDIENTS

- 2 tablespoons light olive oil
- 6 medium onions, peeled and chopped
- 6 garlic cloves, peeled and chopped
- 3½ pounds ground bison/buffalo meat
- 2 (28-ounce) cans seasoned diced *tomatoes
- 3 tablespoons chopped fresh opal basil
- 1 tablespoon dried red chili pepper flakes
- ½ teaspoon *Syrian allspice (*for recipe)
- 1 teaspoon dried oregano
- 5 cups tomato sauce
- 1 (12-ounce) can tomato paste
- 1 teaspoon sea salt (optional)
  Cooked pasta (*al dente*—cooked but firm), amount to accommodate the group being served. Suggested amount: 2 pounds for up to 12 people.

---

* See Ingredient Index

INGREDIENTS

1½	tablespoons light olive oil
3	medium onions, peeled and chopped
5	garlic cloves, peeled and chopped
2½	pounds ground bison/buffalo meat
2	(28 ounces) cans seasoned diced *tomatoes
2	(12 ounces) cans tomato paste
7	ounces light beer
3	teaspoons crushed, dried red pepper flakes
½	teaspoon cayenne (or *Mombassa)
½	teaspoons light chili powder
4	teaspoons ground cumin
3	cups black beans (canned or cooked), rinsed and drained
¼	teaspoon Tabasco
	Dash of sea salt

* See Ingredient Index

HOT AND SPICY BLACK BEAN CHILI

Serve this crowd pleaser with hot corn bread and a crisp green salad. Hot and Spicy Black Bean Chili is chock full of protein and gusto. Yield: 6–8 servings

DIRECTIONS

In a large casserole, heat the olive oil over medium heat and add the onions and garlic. Sauté until transparent.

Add the meat to the pan and brown lightly. Remove any excess liquid from the casserole and discard.

Add to the pan, the diced tomatoes, mix. Add the tomato paste, beer, red pepper, cayenne, chili powder, and cumin.

Continue to cook over low heat for 45 minutes. Add the black beans, Tabasco, and salt. Cook 10–12 minutes or until beans are heated. Adjust seasonings. Serve hot.

CALORIC CHART

418 Calories per Serving:
42.079 g Protein
48.874 g Carbohydrate
6.822 g Total Fat:
    1.567 g Saturated
    1.176 g Monounsaturated
    0.760 g Polyunsaturated

88.047 mg Cholesterol
509.000 mg Sodium
9.640 mg Iron

Opposite page:
Photo: Fred Ferris

CHINESE STEAMED BISON DUMPLINGS

INGREDIENTS

▲▲▲▲▲▲▲▲▲

FOR THE DOUGH
- 3 cups all purpose flour
- 1 teaspoon *mugwort *or* *spinach powder (either will make the dumplings green) (optional)
- ⅔ cup boiling water (more if necessary)
- ⅓ cup cold water

FOR THE FILLING
- ¾ pound nappa (Chinese cabbage)
- 1½ pound ground bison/buffalo meat
- 2 teaspoons fresh ginger, peeled and chopped
- 2 green onions, chopped
- 10 *shiitake mushrooms, dried, reconstituted *or* fresh
- ½ teaspoon crushed Asian red pepper
- 1 teaspoon Chinese 5 spices
- 2 garlic cloves, peeled and minced
- 2 teaspoons light sodium-reduced soy sauce
- 2 teaspoons fine sea salt
- 2 teaspoons sesame oil
- Flour for dusting board
- No-stick cooking spray

FOR THE DIPPING SAUCE
(Yield: ½ cup of sauce—you can double, triple, or quadruple the recipe)
- 2 teaspoons white vinegar
- ¼ cup light sodium-reduced soy sauce
- ½ teaspoon sesame oil
- 2 garlic cloves, peeled and minced
- 2 teaspoons ginger root, peeled and minced

_____

* See Ingredient Index

Flavorful and light, these interesting "pillows" filled with buffalo, nappa, and mushrooms are great as either appetizers or as a main course. Serve them as an entree with steamed rice or deep fried if you're not watching your fat intake.   Yield: 4 dozen 3-inch dumplings

DIRECTIONS

▲▲▲▲▲▲▲▲

FOR THE DOUGH

(If adding mugwort or spinach powder, add to the flour and process before adding the liquid.)

In the bowl of a food processor fitted with a steel S blade, add boiling water to the flour and process. Add cold water and process. When the dough forms a ball, remove the dough and let stand for 15 minutes wrapped in a damp (not wet) dish towel.

FOR THE FILLING

In a large pot, parboil the cabbage and set aside to cool.

Place the raw bison meat, ginger, green onion, shiitake mushrooms, Asian red pepper, Chinese 5 spices, minced garlic, soy sauce, salt, and oil in a bowl and mix thoroughly. Lightly squeeze out the water from the parboiled cabbage. Chop the cabbage and add to the meat mixture.

PUTTING THE DUMPLINGS TOGETHER

Remove the dough to a floured board and knead for 2 minutes. Divide the dough into 48 pieces (walnut sized). Flatten each piece with the palm of your hand and roll into thin circles (3 or 4 inches in diameter).

Place a tablespoon of the filling (or more depending on your circle size) in the center of the circle, fold in half, making sure that the filling does not touch the edges. Pinch edges together, forming a crescent shape.

Lightly spray bamboo steamers with no-stick cooking spray. Place the dumplings on each tray (do not let the crescents touch each other) and stack the trays in the wok as high as you have steamers. Pour the remaining water into the wok, until the water level is just below the bottom steamer.

Place the wok with steamers on the stove over high heat and let the dumplings steam for approximately 15 minutes or until the dough appears transparent.

Prepare the dipping sauce.

Continued

DIRECTIONS

(CONTINUED)

FOR THE DIPPING SAUCE

Place the vinegar, soy sauce, sesame oil, garlic, and ginger root in the bowl of a food processor and process until smooth.

CALORIC CHART

302 Calories per Serving:

24.601 g Protein
41.530 g Carbohydrate
3.616 g Total Fat:

0.889 g Saturated
1.244 g Monounsaturated
1.007 g Polyunsaturated

52.828 mg Cholesterol
757.000 mg Sodium
4.925 mg Iron

BISON, WILD RICE, AND SEED STUFFED PUMPKIN

Visually stunning and equally delectable, the stuffing bakes right in the pumpkin. Serve in wedges to your eager guests. A perfect dish to serve in the fall when pumpkins are at their peak.   Yield: 6 servings

DIRECTIONS

Cut the top off of the pumpkin (as you would with a jack-o-lantern). Remove the seeds and stringy fibers and rinse. Prick the cavity of the pumpkin with a fork. Rub the interior of the pumpkin with sea salt and honey mustard. Set aside.

Preheat the oven to 325 degrees.

In a large skillet, add olive oil and heat. Add the onion, leeks, garlic, and green chilies. Sauté until the onions and leeks appear transparent.

Add the meat to the skillet and lightly brown. Remove any excess liquid from the skillet and discard. Add the pumpkin seeds and wild rice to the skillet, mix thoroughly. Add in the sage, thyme, parsley, salt, and pepper (to taste).

Stuff the prepared, hollow pumpkin with the skillet ingredients (the stuffing should come to the top).

In a low shallow pan, add 1½ inches of water and place the stuffed pumpkin into the pan. Cover the top of the stuffing with a piece of aluminum foil to keep it from becoming too browned.

Bake the pumpkin 1½–2 hours or until the pumpkin shell is soft.

Remove the stuffed pumpkin from the oven and carefully transfer it to a plate or platter. Serve each portion in slices, giving each serving pumpkin as well as stuffing.

INGREDIENTS

1	(4–5 pounds) cooking pumpkin
	Sea salt
1½	tablespoons honey mustard
1	tablespoon light olive oil
1	medium onion, peeled and chopped
1	leek, ends cut and chopped
3	garlic cloves, peeled and chopped
2	fresh hot green chilies, stems removed, seeded, and diced (wear rubber gloves!)
1	pound ground buffalo/bison meat
½	cup roasted pumpkin seeds, shelled
1	cup *wild rice (cooked according to package directions)
1	teaspoon powdered sage
2	teaspoons dried thyme
½	cup chopped fresh parsley
	Sea salt
	Black pepper, freshly ground

*See Ingredient Index

CALORIC CHART

313 Calories per Serving:
24.508 g Protein
44.279 g Carbohydrate
5.555 g Total Fat:
      1.256 g Saturated
      0.965 g Monounsaturated
      0.877 g Polyunsaturated

46.959 mg Cholesterol
280.000 mg Sodium
6.122 mg Iron

Opposite page:
Photo: Fred Ferris

STUFFED RED AND GREEN SWISS CHARD WITH SWEET AND SOUR SAUCE

Although generally larger, Swiss chard leaves are quite similar to fresh spinach. Available in both red and green, they are excellent when stuffed. This recipe is a gourmet alternative to stuffed sweet and sour cabbage.

Yield: 4 servings

INGREDIENTS

12 large Swiss chard leaves (6 red, 6 green), stems removed and main vein thinned, if necessary
1½ cups natural brown rice
1 tablespoon canola oil
2 garlic cloves, peeled and minced
2 fresh hot green chilies, stems removed, chilies seeded, and chopped (wear rubber gloves!)
2 medium onions, peeled and chopped
1 pound ground bison/buffalo meat
1 teaspoon sumac
1½ teaspoons mint
Dash of sea salt
1 (28-ounce) can seasoned diced *tomatoes
1 cup water
2½ tablespoons raspberry wine vinegar
2 tablespoons sugar
¼ cup honey
1 teaspoon ground ginger (or ground cardamom)
6 whole cardamom pods

---

* See Ingredient Index

CALORIC CHART

612 Calories per Serving:
34.860 g Protein
102.000 g Carbohydrate
7.823 g Total Fat: 1.462 g Saturated
                       3.574 g Monounsaturated
                       2.001 g Polyunsaturated
70.438 mg Cholesterol
630.000 mg Sodium
8.485 mg Iron

DIRECTIONS

In a large pot filled ¾ full with water, bring to a boil. When the water reaches boiling, immerse Swiss chard leaves and let cook several minutes until the color intensifies and leaves are wilted—do not overcook! Drain leaves and set aside to cool.

Cook 1½ cups **raw** natural brown rice according to the package directions. Set aside.

In a large skillet, add the canola oil and brown the minced garlic, minced chilies, and one of the chopped onions. Add the ground meat and brown. Remove any excess liquid from the skillet and discard. Add the sumac, mint, and salt (to taste) to the meat and stir until all flavors mix. Add 1½ cups cooked rice. Set aside the remaining rice for mealtime. Mix the rice and meat thoroughly; remove to a bowl. (Depending on the size of the leaves, you may be able to fill 16 leaves instead of 12.)

Place one Swiss chard leaf on a cutting board, vein side up. Place a tablespoon full of meat/rice mixture onto the center of the leaf, fold sides of the leaf over the filling and roll. Place on a dish, seam side down. Repeat until all 12 leaves are used. (If your leaves are not large, you will be left with meat/rice mixture.)

In a glass bowl, combine the tomatoes, water, vinegar, sugar, honey, ground ginger (or ground cardamom), and whole cardamom.

In the same skillet (other ingredients removed), lightly brown the remaining chopped onion. Place each stuffed Swiss chard leaf in the skillet and lightly brown. Add the tomato mixture and bring to a boil. Reduce the heat and simmer for 1 hour. (Do not let the stuffed leaves become limp—remove sooner if necessary.)

Serve the stuffed Swiss chard (giving each plate mixed colors) over warmed brown rice and spoon sauce from skillet on top.

MEATBALLS WITH
PINE NUT PANADA SAUCE

If meatballs are your passion, you'll love these. Filled with pine nuts and feta cheese, these are rich in Mediterranean flavor. Serve them large for dinner or smaller as hor d'oeuvres at your next soirée.

Yield: 3 dozen (depending on size)

DIRECTIONS

FOR THE MEATBALLS

Heat the canola oil in a skillet and sauté the onions and garlic until golden.

In a bowl, soak the bread crumbs in the milk and squeeze dry. Add the bread crumbs to the skillet and mix thoroughly. When completely mixed, remove from the heat.

Using the food processor with the steel S blade, add the onion, garlic, and bread crumb mixture to the bowl. Process until all ingredients are mixed well. Remove and put in a large mixing bowl. Add the meat, egg whites, feta cheese, parsley, mint, cayenne, salt, cloves, Syrian allspice, cinnamon, and lemon juice. Mix well and refrigerate for 2 hours. Remove from the refrigerator. Make the meat mixture into balls (the size of your choice), lightly dredge them through the sifted flour—shaking off excess flour by tossing from hand to hand.

Heat the oil in a large skillet. Add the floured meatballs to the hot oil (fry a few at a time so you can maintain control). Brown the meatballs on all sides, remove them to paper towels to drain.

Preheat the oven to 325 degrees.

FOR THE SAUCE

In a medium-sized saucepan, add the olive oil and sauté the garlic. Add the pine nuts, continue stirring until slightly browned.

Add the cherry wine, water, beef tea, parsley, and cilantro. Bring to a boil, simmer 8–10 minutes. Slowly add enough bread crumbs to thicken the sauce. Keep in mind that the sauce will thicken as it continues to cook. (Watch the amount of bread crumbs!)

PUTTING IT TOGETHER

Spray a shallow pan with cooking spray. Place the browned meatballs in the pan. Cover the pan and cook in a preheated oven at 325 degrees for 30 minutes or until warm. Serve with the sauce on top of the meatballs or on the side.

INGREDIENTS

FOR THE MEATBALLS

1	tablespoon canola oil
3	medium onions, peeled and chopped
4	garlic cloves, peeled and minced
1	cup plain bread crumbs—preferably made from calorie-reduced bread
½	cup skim milk
2	pounds ground bison/buffalo meat
5	egg whites
½	cup low-fat feta cheese, crumbled
½	cup chopped fresh parsley
¼	cup chopped fresh mint
½	teaspoon cayenne (or *Mombassa)
1	teaspoon sea salt
½	teaspoon ground cloves
½	teaspoon *Syrian allspice (*for recipe)
½	teaspoon ground cinnamon
2	tablespoons fresh lemon juice
	Sifted flour for dredging meatballs
	Canola oil (as little as possible)
	No-stick cooking spray

FOR THE SAUCE

1	tablespoon light olive oil
3	garlic cloves, peeled and minced
½	cup pine nuts
1½	cups cherry wine
1⅜	cups water
⅛	cup *plus* ⅛ teaspoon *beef tea
1	tablespoon dried parsley
1	tablespoon dried cilantro
	Herb-seasoned stuffing mix processed to bread crumbs (used to thicken sauce)

* See Ingredient Index

CALORIC CHART

118 Calories per Meatball:		
8.203 g Protein		
9.996 g Carbohydrate		
3.984 g Total Fat:	0.977 g Saturated	
	1.471 g Monounsaturated	
	0.888 g Polyunsaturated	
18.481 mg Cholesterol		
202.000 mg Sodium		
1.399 mg Iron		

RAMEKINS OF FRUITED BUFFALO

These individual ramekins are a great do-ahead dinner. Make the ramekins the day before and bake them fresh for your guests. The unusual combination of buffalo, dried fruits, and nuts make this an interesting—and impressive—main course.   Yield: 6 servings

INGREDIENTS

- 2 tablespoons light olive oil
- 2 large onions, peeled and chopped
- 3 large garlic cloves, peeled and chopped
- 1½ cups bread crumbs (preferably homemade) (do **not** use Italian flavored)
- 1 cup ½% milk
- 2 egg whites
- ⅔ cup water
- ½ cup dried *cherries
- 2 pounds ground bison/buffalo meat
- 2 tablespoons curry powder
  Juice of two lemons (6 tablespoons)
- 2 ounces blanched almonds, chopped
- ¾ cup mango or any fruited chutney
- ¼ teaspoon cayenne (or *Mombassa)
  Dash of sea salt
  No-stick cooking spray

* See Ingredient Index

DIRECTIONS

Preheat the oven to 325 degrees.

In a large skillet, heat the oil over medium-high heat and add the chopped onion and garlic. Cook until browned.

In a glass bowl, soak the bread crumbs in the milk. Squeeze dry, reserving milk, and remove the bread crumbs to a small bowl. To the reserved milk, add the egg whites.

In a small saucepan, add the water and dried cherries. Let the cherries cook until soft; drain the cherries.

In a large bowl, combine the raw ground buffalo, bread crumbs, onion, garlic, cherries, curry powder, lemon juice, almonds, chutney, cayenne, and salt (to taste), mix thoroughly. Add the milk/egg mixture, combine all ingredients.

Lightly spray the (6) 10 cm (7½ ounce) ramekins with cooking spray and add the completed meat mixture. Lower the oven temperature to 310–315 degrees and bake the ramekins for 1 hour.

When the meat mixture is cooked and nicely browned, carefully remove any excess liquid that is in the ramekin, either by using a baster or carefully tipping the ramekins on their sides, letting the juices escape.

Optional: While the meat is cooking, prepare natural long-grained white rice. After the rice is completed, add fresh, chopped parsley to the rice and mix. Place one warm ramekin on each dinner-sized plate, circled with white rice and parsley and serve.

CALORIC CHART

	481 Calories per Serving:	
42.053 g Protein		
47.098 g Carbohydrate		
14.952 g Total Fat:		2.834 g Saturated
		4.988 g Monounsaturated
		1.861 g Polyunsaturated
95.584 mg Cholesterol		
309.000 mg Sodium		
6.165 mg Iron		

Photo: Fred Ferris

SWEET BISON
WITH GREEN ONION SANDWICHES

INGREDIENTS

FOR THE SAUCE
- ½ cup prepared bottled chili sauce
- ½ cup seasoned diced *tomatoes, drained
- ¼ cup chopped pitted prunes
- ½ cup water
- 1 teaspoon ground cumin
- 1 teaspoon chili powder
- 1 teaspoon dry Oriental hot mustard powder
- ½ teaspoon Worcestershire sauce
- 2 garlic cloves, peeled and minced
- ¼ cup sugar

FOR THE MEAT
- No-stick cooking spray
- 1 medium Spanish onion, peeled and chopped
- 1 large green pepper, stem removed, pepper seeded, and chopped
- 1½ pounds ground bison/buffalo meat
- ¾ cup thinly sliced green onions

---

* See Ingredient Index

Sloppy Joes never tasted this good—or this healthy! Serve over a thick slice of homemade bread or on a grainy bun. Yield: 4-6 servings

DIRECTIONS

FOR THE SAUCE

Mix together the chili sauce, tomatoes, prunes, water, cumin, chili powder, mustard powder, Worcestershire sauce, garlic, and sugar in a medium-sized saucepan. Cook mixture slowly for 15 minutes, stirring during a low boil.

FOR THE MEAT

As the sauce is cooking, spray a large skillet with cooking spray. Add the onion and lightly sauté the onion until transparent. Add the green pepper and sauté until slightly tender. Add the meat and lightly brown, removing any liquid with a baster.

PUTTING IT TOGETHER

When the meat is cooked, add the sauce and blend thoroughly. Remove the skillet from the heat. Add the green onions to the mixture and serve over a thick slice of bread or on a bun.

CALORIC CHART

297 Calories per Serving:

31.216 g Protein
35.604 g Carbohydrate
3.501 g Total Fat:

0.805 g Saturated
0.952 g Monounsaturated
0.275 g Polyunsaturated

70.438 mg Cholesterol
587.000 mg Sodium
4.187 mg Iron

ZITI TAPENADE-CHÈVRE

Unusual sun-dried tomato tapenade transforms this pasta and buffalo dish into a culinary hit. This recipe is light and delicious with no heavy aftertaste. Serve with sautéed rapini and crunchy bruschetta.   Yield: 6 servings

DIRECTIONS

In a large skillet, heat the light olive oil over medium-high heat. Add the shallots and elephant garlic. Cook until soft, about 8–10 minutes. Add the wine and simmer for 5 minutes more. Add the mushrooms and peppers. Cook approximately another 5 minutes, until the mushrooms appear cooked and the peppers are still crisp. Remove the skillet from the heat.

In a small skillet, cook the ground buffalo over medium-high heat until no longer pink. Discard any liquid in the pan. Set the meat aside. Add the meat to the vegetable mixture in the large skillet.

In a large pot, cook the ziti in rapidly boiling water until *al dente* (cooked, but firm), test after 7–10 minutes.

Drain the pasta thoroughly and place in a large bowl. Add the vegetable/meat mixture to the pasta. Add the chopped sun-dried tomatoes, sun-dried tomato paste, and Chèvre cheese. Mix, making sure that all ingredients are incorporated. Serve warm.

CALORIC CHART

609 Calories per Serving:	
28.698 g Protein	
88.740 g Carbohydrate	
15.947 g Total Fat:	1.867 g Saturated
	2.168 g Monounsaturated
	0.835 g Polyunsaturated
41.973 mg Cholesterol	
108.000 mg Sodium	
6.942 mg Iron	

INGREDIENTS

3	tablespoons light olive oil
8	shallots, peeled and finely chopped
2	large pieces elephant garlic, peeled and finely chopped
½	cup medium dry red wine (red table wine)
4	very large fresh button mushrooms, stems removed, mushrooms thinly sliced
2	chocolate peppers or red peppers, stems removed, seeded, and cut into bite-sized pieces
⅔	pound ground bison/buffalo meat
2	teaspoons dried sweet basil
1	pound ziti (enriched macaroni product)
1	(8-ounce) jar *sun-dried tomatoes in olive oil, drained, patted dry, and chopped *or* 1 (8-ounce) jar *Dried Tomato Tapenade, drained and patted dry
2	tablespoons *sun-dried tomato paste
6	ounces Chèvre cheese (goat's milk cheese)

* See Ingredient Index

BISON KUGEL WITH DRIED CHERRIES

INGREDIENTS

▲▲▲▲▲▲▲▲▲

1 package (12 ounces) cholesterol-free egg noodles with no yolks
1½ large Spanish onion, peeled and chopped
1½ tablespoons canola oil
1¾ pounds ground bison/buffalo meat
3 tablespoons *beef tea
1 cup dried *cherries
¼ cup dried parsley
1½ teaspoons onion salt
12 egg whites
No-stick cooking spray
½ cup ground multi-bran square cereal

---

* See Ingredient Index

Traditionally, kugels may be either sweet or savory. Bison kugel is both. Using cholesterol free noodles and egg whites only, this kugel is healthy as well. Bison kugel freezes well for up to one month.   Yield: 6-8 servings

DIRECTIONS

▲▲▲▲▲▲▲▲

Preheat the oven to 325 degrees.

In a large pot, bring four quarts of water with a drop of canola oil to a rapid boil. Add the entire package of noodles to the water, stirring to separate the noodles. Cook until *al dente* (cooked, but firm). Drain and rinse the noodles with cold water.

In a large skillet over medium-high heat, sauté the chopped onions in canola oil until they are transparent. Add the ground bison and cook until browned. Drain any excess liquid with a baster and discard.

Add the beef tea to the meat mixture and mix thoroughly. Remove the meat to a large mixing bowl.

To the mixing bowl, fold in the cooked noodles, dried *cherries, parsley and onion salt. Lightly beat the egg whites and add to the mixture, combine thoroughly.

Spray an 8 x 10 inch rectangular baker or any other shallow 9 x 13 x 2 inch pan with cooking spray. Add the meat and noodle mixture, top lightly with ground multi-bran cereal.

Bake 45 minutes to 1 hour or until the top is browned. Check the pan at 45 minutes.

---

* Dried blueberries, cranberries, or any other dried fruit of your choice may be substituted for dried cherries.

CALORIC CHART

▲▲▲▲▲▲▲▲▲▲

368 Calories per Serving:
40.047 g Protein
74.935 g Carbohydrate
6.554 g Total Fat: 1.000 g Saturated
                                      2.369 g Monounsaturated
                                      1.124 g Polyunsaturated

61.633 mg Cholesterol
413.000 mg Sodium
4.980 mg Iron

INGREDIENTS

FOR THE DOUGH

2	cups sifted all-purpose flour
¼	teaspoon sea salt
½	teaspoon baking powder
¼	cup canola oil
2	egg whites
6	tablespoons warm water (use more if needed)
	Flour for dusting board
	No-stick cooking spray

FOR THE FILLING

2	cups sweet potatoes, peeled and cubed
1	tablespoon canola oil
1	medium onion, peeled and chopped
1	pound ground bison/buffalo meat
2	egg whites
¼	teaspoon cinnamon
¼	teaspoon nutmeg
¼	teaspoon *Syrian allspice (*for recipe)
	Dash of sea salt

_____

* See Ingredient Index

CALORIC CHART

88.078 Calories per Serving:
4.973 g Protein
10.747 g Carbohydrate
2.679 g Total Fat: 0.292 g Saturated
                       1.453 g Monounsaturated
                       0.752 g Polyunsaturated
9.392 mg Cholesterol
60.592 mg Sodium
1.028 mg Iron

SWEET POTATO AND BUFFALO KNISHES

I've taken the conventional Jewish turnover recipe and turned it into a healthy, yet scrumptious, appetizer or main dish. I've also changed the filling to reflect my personal tastes...meat and sweet potatoes are combined with cinnamon, nutmeg, and allspice for a sweeter, spicier version.

Yield: 1–2½ dozen (depending upon the size you choose)

DIRECTIONS

FOR THE DOUGH

In the bowl of a food processor fitted with a steel S blade, pour in the flour, salt, and baking powder. Add the oil, egg whites, and water, process for 10 seconds. Add more water (if needed) and continue to process until the dough forms into a ball. The dough will appear a bit sticky. Remove the dough from the processor bowl and place it into a glass bowl. Cover the bowl with plastic wrap. Rest the dough in a warm spot away from drafts for one hour. While the dough is resting, make the filling.

FOR THE FILLING

Cook the cubed sweet potatoes in water until soft enough to mash with a fork. Place the sweet potatoes into the bowl of a food processor. Using the steel S blade, process until mashed. (This step can be done much earlier or you may use a leftover sweet potato dish if you have one.)

Heat the oil in a skillet over high heat. Add the onions and cook until browned. Reduce the heat to medium and add the ground meat. Cook the meat until browned. Discard any remaining liquid. Remove the meat and onion mixture to a large bowl and add the potatoes, egg whites, cinnamon, nutmeg, Syrian allspice, and salt (to taste). Mix all the ingredients thoroughly and set aside.

PUTTING IT TOGETHER

On a lightly floured board, roll ½ the dough (⅛ of an inch thick). With a cookie cutter or the rim of a glass, cut the dough into rounds (they can be any size keeping in mind their use, either main course or appetizer). Place a spoonful of the filling on each round. Pull the dough around the filling, gathering the dough on top. Push in the center like a belly button.

Spray a baking sheet with cooking spray. Place the knishes belly button side down and bake at 325–350 degrees until golden brown, 45 minutes to 1 hour. Remove the knishes from the oven onto cooling rack. Serve warm.

GOURMET PIZZA

Meaty portabello mushrooms and goat cheese lighten what is usually considered a dietary no-no. Use this pizza dough and sauce recipe and add your favorite topping...the possibilities are endless.   Yield: 4 servings

DIRECTIONS

FOR THE DOUGH

In a small glass container, mix the yeast and water together. In the bowl of a food processor, add the flour, yeast/water mixture, olive oil, and salt. Using the steel S blade, process until the dough forms a ball.

Take the dough out of the food processor bowl. Pat the dough into a ball (dough should feel smooth and elastic). Place the dough ball into a glass bowl and cut an "x" on the top of the ball with a sharp knife. Cover the bowl with plastic wrap and put in a warm spot free from drafts for 2 hours or until the dough has doubled in size.

FOR THE TOPPING

While the dough is rising, spray a large skillet with cooking spray. Over medium-high heat, lightly brown the ground buffalo.

In a small cup, mix together the sun-dried tomato paste and anchovy paste. Cover with plastic wrap and set aside.

Wash and cut the mushrooms. In a skillet, sauté the mushrooms in wine for about 6 minutes or until tender (do not let them get too well done). Drain the mushrooms.

Drain the tomatoes and place in a bowl.

PUTTING THE PIZZA TOGETHER

Remove the dough from the bowl. Place the dough on a lightly floured board, knead slightly with hands for 30 seconds. Roll out the dough to the approximate shape of the pizza pan.

Spray the pizza pan with cooking spray (pizza pans with small holes across the surface are the best for uniform heat).

Place the dough on the pan, pushing with your fingers to get it to spread all the way to the edge. The crust can be thick or thin; you will have enough dough to have your choice.

Smooth the surface of the pizza dough with your hands. Brush on the sun-dried tomato/anchovy paste and sprinkle with fresh basil. Add the diced tomatoes, mushrooms, ground buffalo, and cheeses.

Bake at 375 degrees for approximately 45 minutes or until pizza is done (as desired). Let the pizza sit for a few minutes for cutting ease. (Kitchen scissors work great!) Serve warm.

INGREDIENTS

FOR THE DOUGH

1	package fast rise *yeast
1	cup *plus* 1 tablespoon warm water
3½	cups all purpose flour
2	tablespoons light olive oil
	Dash of coarse sea salt

FOR THE TOPPING

	No-stick cooking spray
8	ounces ground bison/buffalo meat
2	tablespoons sun-dried tomato paste
1	teaspoon anchovy paste
5	fresh medium-sized *portabello mushrooms, cut into slices
2	cups seasoned diced *tomatoes, drained Flour for dusting board
1–2	tablespoons chopped fresh basil, stems removed
2	ounces crumbled low-fat feta cheese
4	ounces crumbled Chèvre cheese (goat's milk cheese)

* See Ingredient Index

CALORIC CHART

680 Calories per Serving:
31.354 g Protein
95.088 g Carbohydrate
16.779 g Total Fat: 3.743 g Saturated
                        1.257 g Monounsaturated
                        0.741 g Polyunsaturated
60.686 mg Cholesterol
551.000 mg Sodium
8.772 mg Iron

GIRELLINI DE RICOTTA-BISON-CHÈVRE

▲▲▲▲▲▲▲▲▲▲▲◇▲▲▲▲▲▲▲▲▲▲▲

This roulade is luscious and elegant and well worth the extra effort. Serve this on a special occasion for two or for twenty. It's just as delicious made the day before and baked just before serving.   Yield: 8 servings

Special equipment needed—a large fish poacher or a pan that can accommodate boiling a long pasta roll

INGREDIENTS

FOR THE PASTA

2¼	cups pre-sifted flour
4	egg whites
2	tablespoons light olive oil
1	tablespoon white or blush wine
1-2	tablespoons flat parsley
1	tablespoon water
	Flour for dusting board

FOR THE FILLING

	No-stick cooking spray
⅔	pound ground bison/buffalo meat
½	pound Swiss chard leaves, cooked and drained (you may substitute spinach if you are unable to find Swiss chard)
15	ounces low-fat/part skim ricotta cheese
2	ounces Chèvre cheese (goat's milk cheese)
1	cup shredded low-fat mozzarella cheese
4	egg whites
½	teaspoon sea salt
¼	teaspoon ground cayenne (or *Mombassa)

FOR THE SAUCE

1	(28-ounce) can *tomato sauce
1½	teaspoons dried oregano

* See Ingredient Index

DIRECTIONS

▲▲▲▲▲▲▲▲

FOR THE PASTA

In a food processor bowl, add the flour, egg whites, olive oil, wine, parsley, and water. Using a steel S blade, process until the pasta dough forms a ball on top of the blade (this means pasta dough is all kneaded and ready). Remove the dough and wrap it in plastic wrap and place it in the refrigerator until needed.

FOR THE FILLING

Spray a large skillet with cooking spray. Lightly brown the meat.

Place the washed Swiss chard into a saucepan and cover with water. Bring to a boil and cook over high heat until tender and deep in color, drain the Swiss chard and squeeze out all of the excess water.

In a clean food processor bowl using a steel S blade, place the cheeses, egg whites, Swiss chard, salt, and pepper. Process until well blended. Add the browned meat—use the pulse button, keeping the meat from becoming too mushy. Set aside temporarily.

PUTTING IT TOGETHER

On a floured board, roll out the dough thin and rectangular. Spread the filling evenly across the pasta dough. Carefully roll the dough up like a jelly roll (pasta should be approximately 22 inches in length), tuck in ends.

Using a fish poacher, boil water (about ½ full). Spray the poacher insert with cooking spray. Gently place the long filled pasta roll onto insert, seam side down.

When the water comes to a rapid boil, gently submerge the pasta roll into the water and lower the heat to a light boil. Cook 8–10 minutes (making sure the pasta is *al dente*—cooked, but firm). Lift the poacher insert out of the water by its handles. Turn off the heat and let the pasta drain slightly by placing the insert tilted across the poacher bottom.

Slide the roll off the poacher insert onto a table or board to cool.

Continued on page 66

Opposite page:
Photo: Fred Ferris

GIRELLINI DE RICOTTA-BISON-CHEVRE

DIRECTIONS
(CONTINUED)

▲▲▲▲▲▲▲▲▲

FOR THE SAUCE

Spray a 10 x 14 inch rectangular baker or a large, low pan of equal size with cooking spray. Spoon a light film of tomato sauce on the bottom of the pan. When cool, cut the pasta roll into ¾ inch slices, one at a time. Turning it to the side (open end up), lift the slices with a narrow metal spatula and place girellini side by side in the pan. Cover the pasta slices with a light coat of tomato sauce and sprinkle with oregano lightly on top.

Bake at 350 degrees on the upper rack of the oven for approximately 30 minutes or until steaming. Serve warm.

CALORIC CHART

▲▲▲▲▲▲▲▲▲▲

375 Calories per Serving:

28.574 g Protein
36.801 g Carbohydrate
11.355 g Total Fat:

    4.433 g Saturated
    1.534 g Monounsaturated
    0.362 g Polyunsaturated

42.623 mg Cholesterol
837.000 mg Sodium
3.707 mg Iron

AEGEAN GROUND BISON AND PASTA

The taste of this region is truly evident in this pasta dish. I recommend using a spicy, fanciful shaped pasta...it's so much more fun.   Yield: 6-8 servings

DIRECTIONS

Cook the pasta in a large pot of boiling water with a drop of oil added to keep the noodles separated. Boil the noodles until *al dente* (cooked, but firm). Drain the pasta and set aside.

Heat 1½ tablespoons of oil in a heavy skillet. Add the onions and garlic. Sauté the onions until lightly browned. Add the ground meat and brown. Drain any excess liquid. Add the oregano, parsley, nutmeg, cinnamon, pepper, and sun-dried tomato bits. Add the white wine and continue to cook over low heat for 8 minutes. Let the skillet ingredients cool slightly.

Remove the meat to a bowl, add the drained tomatoes, cooked and drained pasta, and the grated fresh Parmesan cheese—toss gently.

FOR THE SAUCE

In a small bowl, mix the chicken bouillon and the evaporated milk.

Heat a small saucepan. Add the flour and pepper, stir with a whisk for several minutes, then gradually add the milk mixture. Continue to stir the milk mixture until it becomes slightly thickened (approximately 10–12 minutes). Let cool for 5 minutes and add to the bowl with the rest of the ingredients, mix.

PUTTING IT TOGETHER

Preheat the oven to 350 degrees.

Lightly spray a large 10 x 14 inch rectangular baker, or any other shallow pan, with no-stick cooking spray; pour in the bison and pasta mixture.

Bake for 20–30 minutes or until the milk mixture appears to be set and the top is lightly browned. Remove from the oven and let stand for a few minutes before serving.

CALORIC CHART

	390 Calories per Serving:	
27.152 g Protein		
48.686 g Carbohydrate		
7.845 g Total Fat:	2.719 g Saturated	
	2.915 g Monounsaturated	
	0.996 g Polyunsaturated	
45.319 mg Cholesterol		
656.000 mg Sodium		
3.563 mg Iron		

INGREDIENTS

1½   tablespoons canola oil
12   ounces of pasta—*Spicy Spirals (or any other type and shape of pasta)
1   medium Spanish onion, peeled and chopped
4   large garlic cloves, peeled and chopped
1   pound ground bison/buffalo meat
1   teaspoon dried oregano
2   tablespoons chopped fresh parsley
¼   teaspoon nutmeg
½   teaspoon ground cinnamon
     Sea salt
     Black pepper, freshly ground
1   tablespoon *sun-dried tomato bits
⅝   cup dry white wine
1   (28-ounce) can seasoned diced *tomatoes, drained
3   ounces freshly grated Parmesan cheese
     No-stick cooking spray

FOR THE SAUCE
½   cup prepared chicken bouillon
1   (12-ounce) can light evaporated milk
¼   cup pre-sifted flour
⅛   teaspoon freshly ground peppercorn mélange

* See Ingredient Index

CURRIED RED LENTIL, PUMPKIN, AND BISON CHILI

This soup is so thick and hearty, I've labeled it a chili. Hot, spicy, and filling, it's perfect on a chilly winter's night or whenever you feel like good "comfort food" with a zing.   Yield: 8-10 plus servings

DIRECTIONS

Heat the oil in a large casserole over medium-high heat. Add the onions, garlic, and green chilies. Cook until the onions are transparent. Add the chopped carrots and continue to sauté until the carrots and other vegetables are lightly browned (do not let them burn). Reduce heat.

Add the pumpkin and sauté for 2–3 minutes. Add the red lentils and sauté until all the ingredients are mixed.

Add the water, brown sugar, curry powder, turmeric, and coriander seed. Cook about 15 minutes more. Add the raisins. Stir the soup periodically to mix the ingredients and prevent sticking to the bottom of the pot.

While those ingredients are cooking, in a separate pan, dry brown the ground bison meat removing any liquid that may accumulate. When the meat is browned, turn off the heat and set the meat aside to cool. Once cool, remove it from the pan to a bowl of a food processor fitted with a steel S blade and process for 30 seconds. Set aside.

Continue to cook the soup until the lentils are soft and tender (approximately 1–1½ hours). Once the lentils are tender, adjust spices (if necessary) and add the cooked meat. Stir to mix thoroughly. Serve warm.

CALORIC CHART

<table>
<tr><td colspan="2">265 Calories per Serving:</td></tr>
<tr><td>15.388 g Protein</td><td></td></tr>
<tr><td>48.423 g Carbohydrate</td><td></td></tr>
<tr><td>2.865 g Total Fat:</td><td>0.480 g Saturated</td></tr>
<tr><td></td><td>1.190 g Monounsaturated</td></tr>
<tr><td></td><td>0.643 g Polyunsaturated</td></tr>
<tr><td>21.131 mg Cholesterol</td><td></td></tr>
<tr><td>37.882 mg Sodium</td><td></td></tr>
<tr><td>5.060 mg Iron</td><td></td></tr>
</table>

INGREDIENTS

1	tablespoon canola oil
3	large onions (*Vidalias if possible), peeled and chopped
6	large garlic cloves, peeled and chopped
2	fresh hot green chilies, seeded and chopped
3	large carrots, ends cut, carrots peeled and chopped
2½	cups canned pumpkin
1½	cups small red lentils, sorted well and washed
8	cups water
2½	tablespoons firmly packed light brown sugar
2–4	tablespoons curry powder
1	teaspoon turmeric
1	tablespoon ground coriander seed
1½	cups sultanas (yellow raisins)
¾	pound ground bison/buffalo meat

* See Ingredient Index

Opposite page: Sioux doll, circa 1920.
Courtesy of Mesa Arts. Photo: Fred Ferris

STUFFED BISON BURGERS WITH HOMEMADE OAT BRAN BUNS

Your guests will be deliciously surprised when they bite into these sizzling, jumbo burgers. The work is in the oat bran buns, but certainly well worth the time and effort. Serve with coleslaw and baked—not fried—potato chips.

Yield: 12 servings

INGREDIENTS

FOR THE OAT BRAN BUNS

1½	cups of ½% milk
3	tablespoons light olive oil
2½	teaspoons honey
2	teaspoons sea salt
2½	teaspoons fast rise *yeast
1	teaspoon sugar
½	cup warm water
6	cups bread flour
4	egg whites
¾	cup Oat Bran high fiber hot cereal
	No-stick cooking spray
	Black or white sesame seeds (optional)

FOR THE BISON BURGERS

6	roasted peppers (any type can be used— hot, hotter, hottest, or sweet!)
4½	pounds (72 ounces) ground bison/buffalo meat
12	tablespoons reduced fat, shredded cheese

* See Ingredient Index

DIRECTIONS

FOR THE OAT BRAN BUNS

In a heavy saucepan, scald the milk. Once scalded, add the oil, honey, and salt. Mix gently, set aside momentarily.

In a glass bowl, dissolve the yeast and sugar in ½ cup warm (not hot) water. Stir for several minutes and add the milk mixture.

In the bowl of a large kitchen mixer (with paddle in place), add three cups of flour, egg whites, and milk/yeast mixture and mix. Add the remaining 3 cups of flour and the oat bran. Beat on medium speed until the dough is well mixed. Replace the paddle with a dough hook and continue beating at medium speed until the dough is elastic to the touch and appears ball-like.

Spray a large glass bowl or container with no-stick cooking spray. Place the dough ball in the bowl and cover with plastic wrap. Place the bowl in a warm area free from drafts and let rise approximately 1 hour or until the dough doubles in size.

Once doubled, remove the dough from the bowl, and punch down. Knead by hand on a lightly floured surface for just a minute or two.

Divide the dough into 12 equal portions. Shape into balls and cover with a damp dish towel; let the dough rest for 15–20 minutes.

Lightly spray 2 baking sheets with no-stick cooking spray. Place 6 balls of dough per baking sheet—flatten each ball lightly with the palm of your hand. Lightly spray the top of each dough ball with cooking spray, add sesame seeds if desired.

Place the baking sheets in a warm spot free of drafts and allow the dough to rise again for 30 minutes.

Preheat the oven to 400 degrees.

Bake the buns for 15–20 minutes or until golden brown. Remove them from the oven and place them on a cooling rack.

Cut the buns in half for use.

Continued

70

DIRECTIONS
(CONTINUED)

FOR THE BURGERS

Roast the peppers whole over an open flame, until they are blackened and blistered. Remove the peppers to a glass container and cover it with plastic wrap. When the peppers are cool enough to handle, remove the skin, stem, and seeds and slice the peppers into thin strips. (See *note below.)

Weigh out 24 (3 ounce) patties, keeping all the burgers consistent in size and weight.

On half of the patties (12), place several strips of the roasted pepper and a tablespoon of the shredded cheese. Place a plain patty on top and close the burgers by gently pinching the edges and patting it all around. (The patties may open slightly during cooking as there is so little fat to keep them together.)

Grill the burgers to desired doneness; an indoor grill works extremely well! Place the burgers on their buns and supply condiments.

CALORIC CHART

527 Calories per Serving:	
50.104 g Protein	
57.462 g Carbohydrate	
9.964 g Total Fat:	3.040 g Saturated
	1.412 g Monounsaturated
	1.022 g Polyunsaturated
112.000 mg Cholesterol	
517.000 mg Sodium	
7.596 mg Iron	

*Note: See Ingredient Index for more detailed instructions (under ROASTING FRESH PEPPERS OR CHILES)

MISCELLANEOUS
BISON RECIPES

GRILLED BUFFALO SAUSAGE SALAD
WITH STRAWBERRY VINAIGRETTE

The combination of grilled sausage and the delicate, berry dressing make this distinctive salad a fine choice for luncheons and elegant suppers.

Yield: 4–6 servings

INGREDIENTS

FOR THE SALAD

1	pound bison/buffalo sausage
1	head green leaf lettuce
2	fresh beets, peeled, boiled until tender but firm, and cut into ¾-inch pieces
1	yellow bell pepper, cored, seeded, and cut into ¾-inch pieces
6	large fresh mushrooms, stems removed, mushrooms washed and thinly sliced

FOR THE VINAIGRETTE DRESSING

6	tablespoons light olive oil
1	large garlic clove, peeled
1	tablespoon *strawberry wine vinegar
3	large frozen strawberries (frozen berries make the dressing thick and creamy)
¼	cup prepared chicken bouillon

* See Ingredient Index

DIRECTIONS

FOR THE SALAD

Grill or dry pan-fry the bison/buffalo sausage. Once cool, slice it into thin pieces. (If you are going to dry pan-fry it, heat the skillet first.)

Prepare the salad: Wash the leaf lettuce in salty water, then rinse it with clean water until all salt residue is removed. (Leaf lettuce tends to be very dirty and buggy; using the salt aids in cleaning it.) Gently tear the leaves into sections and pat them dry. Refrigerate the leaves until you are ready to use them. Peel and boil the beets until tender but still firm. Cut the beets and bell pepper into ¾ inch pieces; slice the mushrooms.

FOR THE DRESSING

Prepare the salad dressing by placing the olive oil, garlic, strawberries, and chicken bouillon into the bowl of a food processor or blender, blend thoroughly. The salad dressing will yield nearly a cup.

PUTTING IT TOGETHER

Toss the sliced sausage, lettuce, beets, bell pepper, and sliced mushrooms. Serve the "dressing" on the side, leaving the amount to the discretion of the individual (generally two tablespoons per serving).

CALORIC CHART

230 Calories per Serving:

17.700 g Protein	
5.116 g Carbohydrate	
15.784 g Total Fat:	2.614 g Saturated
	0.629 g Monounsaturated
	0.268 g Polyunsaturated
51.642 mg Cholesterol	
130.000 mg Sodium	
2.739 mg Iron	

BISON TONGUE
WITH BLACKBERRY SAUCE

Tangy, sweet, and tart. The addition of fresh blackberries and blackberry wine elevate this entree into a show-stopper. Roasted new potatoes are an excellent accompaniment to this dish.   Yield: 6–8 servings

DIRECTIONS

FOR THE BISON TONGUE

Wash the tongue well in cool water. Place the tongue into a large casserole and cover with cold water. Add the garlic. Bring the water to a quick boil over high heat. Lower the heat to medium and simmer for 2½–4 hours depending on the size of the tongue. Simmer the tongue until tender.

Prepare the blackberry sauce.

FOR THE BLACKBERRY SAUCE

Place the washed and cut blackberries, blackberry wine, sugar, cloves, and cinnamon sticks in a medium saucepan over medium-high heat. Set aside 1 teaspoon of the liquid.

In a small bowl dissolve the cornstarch in 2 tablespoons of water. Stir in the teaspoon of warmed blackberry liquid from the saucepan.

When the berries and wine mixture have cooked about 10–12 minutes (to a boil), add the cornstarch mixture, stirring slowly and constantly until the sauce is thickened. Remove the cinnamon sticks. Set the sauce aside.

PUTTING IT TOGETHER

When the tongue is tender, remove it from the water and drain (reserving the liquid). Cool the tongue under cold running water until you are able to handle it.

When cool enough to handle, with a small sharp knife, skin the tongue (removing any visible fat, bone, or gristle). Carve the tongue diagonally starting at the tip.

Reheat the reserved liquid from the tongue. Place the slices in warmed liquid to regain just enough heat for serving.

Serve the tongue with warm blackberry sauce over each slice.

INGREDIENTS

FOR THE BISON TONGUE

 1   bison/buffalo tongue (2–3 pounds)
 4   whole garlic cloves, peeled

FOR THE BLACKBERRY SAUCE

     (Yield: approximately 2 cups)
 1   pint large blackberries, cut into ½s or ⅓s depending on size of berries
 ¾   cup 100% pure blackberry wine
 1   tablespoon sugar
 8   whole cloves
 2   cinnamon sticks
 1   tablespoon cornstarch
 2   tablespoons water

CALORIC CHART

188 Calories per Serving:
24.840 g Protein
10.246 g Carbohydrate
2.250 g Total Fat: 0.807 g Saturated
0.857 g Monounsaturated
0.288 g Polyunsaturated
70.438 mg Cholesterol
63.646 mg Sodium
3.248 mg Iron

PESTO PASTA
WITH GRILLED BUFFALO SAUSAGE

INGREDIENTS

▲▲▲▲▲▲▲▲▲

3 cups bow-tie or spiral noodles
3 cups bison/buffalo sausage
5 ounces dried *cremini mushrooms,
    reconstituted and sliced

FOR THE SAUCE
¼ cup prepared chicken bouillon
½ cup light olive oil
4 garlic cloves, peeled
2 cups fresh basil leaves, stems removed
½ cup pine nuts
    Sea salt
    Black pepper, freshly ground
½ cup freshly grated Parmesan cheese

---

* See Ingredient Index

This delicious and flavorful pasta is perfect on a buffet served with a crunchy green salad and crusty breadsticks. Or serve it as either a side salad or a summer main course on a hot summer evening.   Yield: 4–6 servings

DIRECTIONS

▲▲▲▲▲▲▲▲▲

Cook the bow-tie or spiral noodles (following the package directions) until *al dente* (cooked, but firm). Rinse the noodles in cold water and drain well. Set aside.

Grill the buffalo sausage on an outdoor grill making sure not to overcook. Once cool, cut into bite size pieces.

FOR THE SAUCE

In the bowl of a food processor: place the olive oil, garlic, basil leaves, pine nuts, chicken bouillon, and salt and pepper (to taste). Pulse the ingredients until smooth. Add the Parmesan cheese and mix slightly.

PUTTING IT TOGETHER

Combine the cooled pasta, grilled and cooled bison/ buffalo sausage and cremini mushrooms in a large mixing bowl. Add just enough of the sauce to coat the pasta and sausage. Toss lightly (avoid breaking the pasta).

Remove the finished salad to a serving dish (clear glass makes for a lovely presentation). Serve at room temperature for best flavor.

CALORIC CHART

▲▲▲▲▲▲▲▲▲

585 Calories per Serving:
37.882 g Protein
42.380 g Carbohydrate
31.222 g Total Fat:

6.389 g Saturated
4.830 g Monounsaturated
2.792 g Polyunsaturated

111.000 mg Cholesterol
498.000 mg Sodium
6.153 mg Iron

Opposite page:
Photo: Fred Ferris

BISON, BEANS, AND BREW

This is a hearty one-dish meal. Ideal for warming up frosty evenings. Add freshly baked bread and a crisp green salad for a complete winter supper.

Yield: 4–6 servings

INGREDIENTS

2	cups *Anasazi beans
1	very large Spanish onion, peeled and chopped
4	large garlic cloves, peeled and minced
1½	tablespoons canola oil
2	carrots, ends cut, carrots peeled and shredded
1½	pounds bison/buffalo sausage
12	ounces light beer
½	celery root bulb (celeriac)
2	bay leaves
2	tablespoons chopped flat parsley
2	sprigs of fresh thyme, chopped
¼–½	teaspoon cayenne (or *Mombassa)
2	tablespoons light brown sugar
¼	teaspoon nutmeg

* See Ingredient Index

DIRECTIONS

Sort and wash the beans. Place the beans and 6 cups of water into an enameled or nonreactive pot. Quick cook (bring the water and beans to a rapid boil, turn off the heat and let sit for 30 minutes). (Note: Quick cooking usually requires more sitting time; but with the type of beans used in this recipe, it is not necessary.) Return the beans to a light boil for 20 minutes or until tender. Let the beans sit until ready for use.

Heat the oil in a large casserole. Add the onions and garlic and sauté until lightly browned. Add the shredded carrots and sauté for an additional 7–10 minutes. Add the beer, celery root, bay leaves, parsley, thyme, cayenne pepper, brown sugar, and nutmeg and mix all ingredients thoroughly. Add the well-drained beans. Simmer for 30 minutes more. Remove from the heat.

In a skillet, dry pan-fry the sausage until browned. Remove from the heat and cut the sausage into 1-inch pieces.

Add the sausage to the vegetable/bean mixture and cook for several minutes, until all flavors are well blended and the sausage is hot.

Remove the celery root and bay leaves, discard. Serve the bison, beans, and brew warm with crusty bread and salad.

CALORIC CHART

294 Calories per Serving:	
30.595 g Protein	
26.016 g Carbohydrate	
6.134 g Total Fat:	1.147 g Saturated
	2.915 g Monounsaturated
	1.289 g Polyunsaturated
77.463 mg Cholesterol	
141.000 mg Sodium	
5.283 mg Iron	

BISON TONGUE,
VIDALIA ONIONS, AND ASPARAGUS
IN MARINADE

Make this delightful salad with the thinnest asparagus you can find. The interesting shapes complement the spicy marinade. Serve with muffins or scones and a first-course of vegetable consomme.   Yield: 6 servings

DIRECTIONS

FOR THE MARINADE

Place the olive oil, wine vinegar, parsley, garlic, mustard, honey, oregano, basil, mint, salt, and pepper in the bowl of a food processor and process until combined.

FOR THE SALAD

In a pot fitted with a stainless steel basket steamer, lightly steam the asparagus, leaving it quite crisp and bright green. Rinse under cold running water to cool.

In a glass bowl, toss the tongue, onion, and asparagus. Pour the marinade over all the ingredients and cover with plastic wrap.

Place in the refrigerator for 3–4 hours to chill.

Remove the bowl from the refrigerator. Lightly toss the marinated tongue, onion, and asparagus and serve over cleaned, separated Romaine lettuce leaves.

CALORIC CHART

260 Calories per Serving:	
36.738 g Protein	
10.796 g Carbohydrate	
7.980 g Total Fat:	
	1.813 g Saturated
	1.092 g Monounsaturated
	0.516 g Polyunsaturated
93.388 mg Cholesterol	
110.000 mg Sodium	
5.303 mg Iron	

INGREDIENTS

FOR THE MARINADE
½ cup light olive oil
½ cup *cranberry wine vinegar
¼ cup chopped fresh parsley
2 garlic cloves, peeled and minced
1 tablespoon prepared Dijon mustard
1 teaspoon honey
½ teaspoon dried oregano
½ teaspoon dried sweet basil
¼ teaspoon dried mint
   Sea salt
   Black pepper, freshly ground

FOR THE SALAD
1½ cups cooked bison tongue, cut into julienne
1 *Vidalia onion, thinly sliced
2 pounds of fresh thin asparagus, ends removed
   Romaine lettuce leaves

* See Ingredient Index

BISON CABBAGE COMPOTE

▲▲▲▲▲▲▲▲▲▲ ◆ ▲▲▲▲▲▲▲▲▲▲

Rich in color and flavor, this compote is sweet and savory. It's a meal in itself; serve with plenty of piping hot bread.   Yield: 6–8 servings

INGREDIENTS

▲▲▲▲▲▲▲▲▲

1½   pounds bison/buffalo sausage
      No-stick cooking spray
1   medium Spanish onion, peeled and diced
4   garlic cloves, peeled and minced
1   small to medium red/purple cabbage, core removed and cabbage shredded
½   pound (2 large) MacIntosh apples, peeled and diced
1   cup Sultanas (yellow raisins)
6   dried apricots, diced (or more, if desired)
1   pound jar ready-to-eat prunes plus liquid, pits removed and prunes chopped
1   teaspoon fresh grated lemon peel
1   teaspoon fresh grated orange peel
3   cinnamon sticks
1   whole bay leaf
½   teaspoon ground cloves
½   teaspoon powdered ginger
⅓   cup firmly packed dark brown sugar
½   cup raspberry wine vinegar
½   cup water

DIRECTIONS

▲▲▲▲▲▲▲▲▲

Grill the bison sausage or dry pan-fry until cooked and browned. Set aside to cool. Slice the cooled sausage into 1½-inch pieces.

Lightly spray a large casserole with no-stick cooking spray. Add the onions and garlic. Sauté the onions and garlic over medium-high heat until transparent. Add the shredded cabbage and sauté for five minutes more.

Add the apples, raisins, apricots, prunes plus liquid, lemon peel, and orange peel. Sauté mixture for several minutes to combine flavors. Add the cinnamon sticks, bay leaf, cloves, ginger, brown sugar, wine vinegar, and water. Cook until tender, stirring occasionally (30–40 minutes).

Add the cooked sausage and heat until the sausage is warm and the flavors are well blended. Serve bison cabbage compote hot.

CALORIC CHART

▲▲▲▲▲▲▲▲▲

302 Calories per Serving:
20.368 g Protein
53.563 g Carbohydrate
2.118 g Total Fat:

0.689 g Saturated
0.753 g Monounsaturated
0.272 g Polyunsaturated

58.098 mg Cholesterol
106.000 mg Sodium
4.273 mg Iron

Opposite page: Right side: Cylindrical Rawhide case. Tribe: Crow, circa 1875.
Front: Storage bag. Tribe: Yankton Sioux, circa 1875.
Courtesy of Richard Pohrt. Photo: Fred Ferris

SOMEN BUFFALO SALAMI SALAD WITH CURRY VINAIGRETTE

Japanese noodles and exotic vegetables make this delicious salad an interesting contrast in textures. The curry completes the mix of Asian flavors.

Yield: 8–10 servings

INGREDIENTS

FOR THE SALAD

6	ounces dry *Tomoshiraga (Somen noodles)
1	cup bison/buffalo salami, cut into julienne
1	cup *Daikon radish, peeled, sliced very thin, and cut into julienne
¼	cup green onion, thinly sliced
1	cup Asian pea pods, steamed, cooled, and cut into julienne
1	cup *jicama, peeled and cut into julienne
3	carrots, peeled and shredded

FOR THE DRESSING

(Yield: ¾ cup)

6	tablespoons light olive oil
2	shallots, peeled
1	large garlic clove, peeled
¼	cup prepared chicken bouillon
1	tablespoon lemon juice
1½	teaspoons curry powder
	Dash of sea salt

---

* See Ingredient Index

DIRECTIONS

FOR THE SALAD

Cook the somen noodles according to package directions, drain the noodles and cool.

FOR THE DRESSING

Place the light olive oil, shallots, garlic, bouillon, lemon juice, curry powder, and salt (to taste) in the bowl of a food processor. Using the steel S blade, process until smooth.

PUTTING IT TOGETHER

Place the cooked noodles on a large platter or in a large bowl. Add the salami, radish, green onions, pea pods, jicama, and carrots. Serve the dressing on the side.

CALORIC CHART

161 Calories per Serving:

3.642 g Protein
18.101 g Carbohydrate
8.791 g Total Fat:

1.273 g Saturated
0.061 g Monounsaturated
0.124 g Polyunsaturated

1.549 mg Cholesterol
380.000 mg Sodium
0.392 mg Iron

Opposite page: Moccasins. Tribe: Cree, circa 1890.
Courtesy of Richard Pohrt. Photo: Fred Ferris

BUFFALO SALAMI BREAD
WITH ROASTED GARLIC

INGREDIENTS

2½   teaspoons fast rise *yeast

1   cup warm water

2   cups bison/buffalo salami (ground in food processor)

⅔   cup freshly grated Parmesan cheese

2   tablespoons flour for dusting salami and cheese

2   tablespoons canola oil

4   egg whites (at room temperature)

3¾   cups all purpose flour

½   teaspoon ground peppercorn mélange

1½   teaspoons sea salt

   Flour for dusting board

   No-stick cooking spray

   Cornmeal for dusting bread pans

2-3   whole bulbs of fresh garlic (make sure they are firm and the skin is intact)

---

* See Ingredient Index

CALORIC CHART

228 Calories per Serving:
13.334 g Protein
31.583 g Carbohydrate
4.835 g Total Fat: 1.467 g Saturated
      2.049 g Monounsaturated
      0.933 g Polyunsaturated
21.542 mg Cholesterol
415.000 mg Sodium
2.688 mg Iron

*Opposite page: Tobacco bag.
Tribe: Blackfeet, circa 1885.
Courtesy of Richard Pohrt. Photo: Fred Ferris*

Use your imagination with this recipe. This bread is fabulous when used for grilled-cheese sandwiches, terrific with your favorite appetizer recipes or made into unique low- or no-fat cream cheese and vegetable sandwiches. Try the cream cheese version with sliced apples. And what could be better than a toasted slice with additional roasted garlic spread on top?   Yield: 2 loaves—12 servings

DIRECTIONS

FOR THE BUFFALO SALAMI BREAD

In a glass container, add the yeast to the warm water and let sit for 15 minutes.

Process the salami in a food processor using the steel S blade (until coarsely chopped). Remove the salami from the processor bowl and place in a glass container with the grated cheese. Add the 2 tablespoons of flour and lightly mix with a rubber spatula until the ingredients seem well dusted.

To the yeast and water combination, add the oil and egg whites; stir just to mix.

In the food processor bowl, with the steel S blade in place, add the flour, peppercorn mélange, and salt. Add the yeast mixture and process until the dough forms a ball on top of the blade. Add the salami and cheese mixture; process on pulse until the dough is mixed. Remove the ball of dough to a floured board and knead by hand for several minutes.

Spray a good sized glass or porcelain bowl lightly with no-stick cooking spray. Place the dough in the bowl and cover with plastic wrap. Place the bowl in a warm spot free of drafts. Let the dough rise until it has doubled in size (approximately 1½ hours). Remove the dough from the glass bowl and punch down; knead for a couple of minutes and divide into 2 equal loaves.

Lightly spray 2 bread pans with no-stick cooking spray and lightly dust with cornmeal. Place each loaf in a bread pan and cover with plastic wrap. Let the dough rise again for 1 hour. Preheat the oven to 425 degrees.

When the dough has risen again, slash each loaf 3 or 4 times across the top with a sharp knife. Place the loaves in the oven and spray each loaf every few minutes with a water atomizer (like those used for spraying house plants) for the first 15–20 minutes of baking. (The spraying reduces quick browning.)

Reduce the heat to 400 degrees and continue to bake until the loaves are golden brown (approximately 45 minutes). During this process, make the roasted garlic.

FOR THE ROASTED GARLIC (to be used as a spread)

Spray any small ovenproof pan with no-stick cooking spray. Also spray the garlic bulbs (before putting them on the pan) and place them in the oven. Bake them with the bread at 400 degrees for approximately 30–40 minutes or until lightly brown and the cloves are soft.

ROAST
RECIPES

A fruity twist on an old favorite. Serve corned the buffalo with grapefruit glaze as a main dish with potatoes and cabbage or in sandwiches "deli style."

Yield: 8 servings with leftovers

INGREDIENTS

FOR CORNING THE MEAT

4	quarts of water
1	tablespoon *potassium nitrate (saltpeter)
1/4	cup sea salt
1/4	cup sugar
1	ounce *pickling spice (placed into large tea strainer or cheese cloth spice bag)
6	whole garlic cloves, peeled
4–6	bay leaves
4–5	pounds bison/buffalo brisket (room temperature)

FOR COOKING THE MEAT

	The corned brisket
2	bunches of green onions (12 onions, both ends cut)

FOR THE GLAZE

1	(12-ounce) jar *grapefruit marmalade
4½	tablespoons grainy mustard (made with white wine)
1	teaspoon ground coriander seed
½	teaspoon ground galangal

---

* See Ingredient Index

CALORIC CHART

291 Calories per Serving:
32.784 g Protein
30.899 g Carbohydrate
3.185 g Total Fat: 1.032 g Saturated
                     1.097 g Monounsaturated
                     0.285 g Polyunsaturated
93.036 mg Cholesterol
354.000 mg Sodium
4.505 mg Iron

DIRECTIONS

FOR CORNING THE MEAT

In a large nonreactive casserole, add the water, saltpeter, salt, sugar, spice bag filled with pickling spice, garlic, and bay leaves. Heat to a rapid boil. Turn off the heat and let the spiced water cool down to room temperature.

Remove the spice bag. Add the meat to the pot, making sure the liquid is covering all of the meat. Cover the pot with a clean, dry towel and place it in the refrigerator for 12–14 days, turning the meat daily.

FOR COOKING THE MEAT

Remove the bison/buffalo brisket from the brine and rinse under cold running water. Discard the brine and wash the pot the brisket was corning in.

Return the brisket to the cleaned pot and cover with cold water. Over high heat, bring the water to a boil, skimming with a mesh skimmer as frequently as needed to keep the water as clear as possible.

Reduce the heat to simmer. Add 2 bunches of green onions and continue to cook on simmer with the pot covered. Cook until fork-tender (cooking time will vary depending on weight and thickness of the meat). Add enough boiling water (if necessary) to keep the water level above the meat.

While the brisket is cooking, prepare the glaze.

FOR THE GLAZE

In a glass container, mix the marmalade, mustard, coriander seed, and galangal together.

PUTTING IT TOGETHER

When the meat is fork-tender, let it remain in the water until you are ready to glaze and bake it (30 minutes before serving time). Preheat the oven to 325 degrees.

Remove the brisket from the water and place it on an oven-proof dish. Spoon the glaze over the top (you may have remaining glaze that can be heated for additional sauce). Bake the brisket for 30 minutes or until coated and shiny in appearance. Serve warm or at room temperature, sliced to desired thickness.

BISON, BEAN,
AND VEGETABLE TUREEN

Robust and filling, this hearty soup is full of vegetables and a variety of beans. Serve piping hot with a big hunk of whole grain bread and a leafy green salad.

Yield: 12 servings

DIRECTIONS

In a large casserole, heat the canola oil and sauté the onions, chiles, and all the garlic. Cook until the onions are transparent.

Add the diced carrots and sauté for 6 minutes. Add the celery and cabbage and cook ten minutes longer. Add the canned tomatoes, basil, water, and tomato sauce; cook for 40 minutes on low heat.

At the same time—sort, wash, and cook the Anasazi beans in a small pot with enough water to cover the beans. When cooked, drain the beans. Add all the beans, peas, and beef tea to soup. Cook for 30 minutes, covered.

Add the meat, cumin, and salt to taste. Cook 45 minutes on low, covered with a lid.

Add the potatoes and chopped cilantro—cook until the potatoes and meat are tender. This soup is better the longer it cooks—stir occasionally to keep from burning!

CALORIC CHART

	266 Calories per Serving:	
22.911 g Protein		
37.250 g Carbohydrate		
3.706 g Total Fat:		0.683 g Saturated
		1.532 g Monounsaturated
		0.871 g Polyunsaturated
41.505 mg Cholesterol		
448.000 mg Sodium		
5.279 mg Iron		

INGREDIENTS

1½ tablespoons canola oil

2 good sized Spanish onions, peeled, and diced

3 fresh hot green chiles, seeded and diced (wear rubber gloves!)

1 whole bulb elephant garlic, minced

3 garlic cloves, peeled and minced

7 medium-sized carrots, ends cut, peeled, and diced

6 stalks of celery with leaves, diced

4½ cups curly cabbage cut into 1-inch pieces

1 (28-ounce) can seasoned diced *tomatoes

2 tablespoons dried basil

8 cups water

2 cups tomato sauce

1 cup dried *Anasazi beans

2 cups canned red kidney beans, rinsed and drained

1 cup frozen crowder peas

4 tablespoons *beef tea

4 cups of roasted bison/buffalo, cubed (from leftover roast)

1 tablespoon cumin
   Dash of sea salt

2 cups raw potatoes cut into small cubes

½ cup finely chopped, fresh cilantro leaves

---
* See Ingredient Index

91

BONELESS BISON ROAST
WITH CRANBERRY PICKLE

INGREDIENTS

FOR THE ROAST
3–4 pounds boneless bison/buffalo shoulder roast, rolled and tied
2 cups red table wine
No-stick cooking spray
Sea salt
Black pepper, freshly ground

FOR THE CRANBERRY PICKLE
1 bag (2 cups) fresh cranberries
¾ cup *cranberry wine vinegar
½ cup *plus* 1 tablespoon sugar (to be used later)
2 teaspoons mustard seed
½ teaspoon cumin seed
1 teaspoon ground fenugreek
2–3 teaspoons chopped dried red chilies
3 large garlic cloves, peeled and minced
½ teaspoon ginger root, peeled and minced

---

* See Ingredient Index

CALORIC CHART

> 281 Calories per Serving:
> 37.180 g Protein
> 23.634 g Carbohydrate
> 3.478 g Total Fat: 1.188 g Saturated
>   1.386 g Monounsaturated
>   0.364 g Polyunsaturated
> 106.000 mg Cholesterol
> 301.000 mg Sodium
> 5.762 mg Iron

The cranberry pickle is the star of this show. The sweet and tangy combination has a real kick to it. Serve this special dish to guests who crave gutsy fare.

Yield: 6–8 servings

DIRECTIONS

FOR PREPARING THE MEAT

Preheat the oven to 275 degrees.

Place the roast in a glass container and add the red wine. Let the meat marinade for 4–6 hours.

Let the roast come to room temperature. Remove the meat from the marinade and pat dry. Lightly spray the roast with no-stick cooking spray, sprinkle with salt and fresh ground black pepper to taste.

Place the roast on a rack in a shallow pan. Insert a meat thermometer into the thickest part of the roast (or keep an instant read thermometer handy to check internal temperature), cover tightly with foil and place it in the oven. When the meat is 10 degrees below desired temperature (135–145), remove the foil for the last few minutes to brown the roast. Remove the roast from the oven and let it stand 8–10 minutes before slicing. Do not overcook this meat—it should remain in the rare to medium-rare range.

Prepare the cranberry pickle while the roast is cooking.

FOR THE CRANBERRY PICKLE

Cut all of the cranberries in half (not through the stem), and place in a colander. To remove the cranberry seeds, place the colander over a sink and shake it until most of the cranberry seeds have fallen through the holes. Wash the halved berries thoroughly.

In a medium saucepan, add the vinegar, ½ cup sugar, mustard seed, cumin seed, fenugreek, and dried chilies. Bring the mixture to a boil and cook an additional 3 minutes.

Add the raw cranberries, garlic, and minced ginger. Turn the heat on low and cook gently for 3–5 minutes. Add the remaining sugar and mix until the sugar is dissolved. Do not overcook the cranberries—leave crisp!

Remove from the heat. Cool down and serve the cranberry pickle with the roast.

Opposite page: Woodlands bag, circa 1920.
Courtesy of Mesa Arts. Photo: Fred Ferris

BORDEAUX ROAST BISON

The Bordeaux marinade imparts a deep and luxurious flavor to the meat. Serve simply with honey-glazed sweet potatoes or puréed sweet potatoes made with a little milk and a drop of honey.   Yield: 10–12 servings

INGREDIENTS

FOR THE ROAST
4–5 pounds top round bison/buffalo roast
2 tablespoons light olive oil

FOR THE MARINADE
3 cups red Bordeaux wine
2 tablespoons light olive oil
3 garlic cloves, peeled and minced
5 shallots, peeled and minced
2 whole bay leaves
1½ teaspoons dried tarragon
1½ teaspoons dried thyme
3 tablespoons dried parsley
1½ teaspoons raspberry wine vinegar
  Sea salt
  Black pepper, freshly ground

---

* See Ingredient Index

CALORIC CHART

252 Calories per Serving:		
32.926 g Protein		
2.287 g Carbohydrate		
7.479 g Total Fat:	1.717 g Saturated	
	1.089 g Monounsaturated	
	0.287 g Polyunsaturated	
93.917 mg Cholesterol		
174.000 mg Sodium		
4.632 mg Iron		

DIRECTIONS

Place the roast in a large casserole.

Mix wine, olive oil, garlic, shallots, bay leaves, tarragon, thyme, parsley, wine vinegar, salt, and pepper in a glass container and pour over the roast. Cover the casserole with a lid or plastic wrap, and place in the refrigerator for 6 hours or more.

Turn the roast from side to side in the marinade every hour or so.

Let the roast and marinade sit at room temperature for one hour prior to cooking. Remove the roast from the marinade and pat the meat dry. Strain the marinade.

Preheat the oven to 275 degrees.

Place the oil in a **clean** casserole. Brown the roast on all sides. When browned, remove any remaining oil from the pot.

Insert a meat thermometer into the thickest part of the roast (or keep an instant read thermometer handy to check internal temperature) and place 1 cup of strained marinade over the roast. Set aside the additional strained marinade. Cover the roast tightly with foil, and place in the oven. Baste the roast frequently with the pan marinade.

When the meat thermometer reaches the desired temperature (approximately 3½–4 hours), remove the roast from the oven.

135 degrees—rare * 145 degrees—medium-rare * 155 degrees—medium

Do not overcook!

Prior to the roast being complete, heat the remaining marinade in a small saucepan, add a dash of salt, and bring to a boil. Reduce the heat and keep warm.

Remove the cooked roast from the pan, slice, and serve. Use the heated marinade as a sauce. Discard the pan drippings.

PEPPERED-GINGER STIR FRY

Enlist your guests in the preparation of this Asian inspired dish. They'll get a kick out of being "involved" in the cooking process. Serve the stir fry with a big bowl of "sticky rice" or traditional fried rice.　　　Yield: 6 servings

DIRECTIONS

Cut partially frozen meat into thin slices. Set aside at room temperature. Prepare the marinade.

FOR THE MARINADE

Mix the sake, cornstarch, soy sauce, and lemon grass in a glass container. Pour the mixture over the defrosted meat. Let the meat marinate for 1 hour or more.

FOR THE SAUCE

In a bowl, add the soy sauce, sugar, chile peppers, green onions, and water. Mix thoroughly.

PUTTING IT TOGETHER

Heat a seasoned wok over high heat to the point where it just begins to smoke. Add the oil to the wok: Pour it in a circular fashion starting at the top, allowing the oil to coat the sides of the wok as it travels down to the center. When the oil starts to smoke, add the garlic cloves. When they become brown in color, remove them and discard. Add the marinated meat. Cook it quickly, stirring constantly until the meat changes color. Once this occurs, remove the meat from the heat.

To the remaining oil, add the onions and stir fry over high heat until lightly browned. Add the green pepper and minced ginger and stir gently for several minutes. Add the drained, partially cooked yams and stir-fry vegetables until tender. If vegetables appear too dry, splash with sake.

Add the partially cooked meat. Mix together with the vegetables and add the sauce. Stir fry until all the ingredients are well blended. Serve with steamed or fried rice.

CALORIC CHART

281 Calories per Serving:		
26.447 g Protein		
25.326 g Carbohydrate		
7.967 g Total Fat:	1.224 g Saturated	
	4.162 g Monounsaturated	
	1.982 g Polyunsaturated	
70.438 mg Cholesterol		
154.000 mg Sodium		
3.639 mg Iron		

INGREDIENTS

1½ pounds top round bison/buffalo (or any tender roast or steak cut). If using a portion of roast, cut meat into approximately 8 inches long x 3 inches wide. Wrap in plastic wrap (double strength). Partially freeze if doing all in one day or totally freeze and partially defrost the day you are cooking. (This partially frozen state enables easy cutting into very thin strips ⅛–¹⁄₁₆ of an inch and 3 inches long.)

2　yams, ends cut, peeled, and partially boiled

2½　tablespoons canola oil

3　garlic cloves, peeled

1　large onion, peeled and cut into ¾-inch pieces

2　peppers (1 red, 1 green), cored, seeded, and cut into 1½-inch thin strips

6　slices of ginger root, peeled and minced

FOR THE MARINADE

2　tablespoons sake

1　tablespoon cornstarch

2　tablespoons light sodium-reduced soy sauce

1　tablespoon dried lemon grass

FOR THE SAUCE

2　tablespoons light sodium-reduced soy sauce

1　teaspoon sugar

3　fresh hot green chile peppers, seeded, and finely diced (wear rubber gloves!)

5　green onions, ends removed and finely chopped

¼　cup water

The sauce should be prepared before the meat is fully cooked.

CURRIED BISON
WITH SWEET POTATOES

Serve this stew-like dish over brown Basmati rice and a sprinkling of roasted Pepitas (pumpkin seeds). The addition of Laban (heavy strained yogurt), lightens this dish rich in color and flavor.   Yield: 4–6 servings

DIRECTIONS

Heat the oil in a large casserole over medium-high heat. Add the bay leaves, cinnamon sticks, cumin seed, black peppercorns, and onions and lightly brown. Add the garlic, minced ginger, turmeric, cloves, and $\frac{1}{2}$ cup of the water. Stir gently for approximately 6–8 minutes.

Add the bison meat and a dash of salt; stir with a slotted spoon until the meat is browned on all sides. Add carrots and sauté. Add $\frac{1}{2}$ cup of the water and ground ginger.

In a medium bowl, mix together the Laban and $\frac{1}{2}$% milk; add to the meat mixture. Cover the casserole and let all these ingredients simmer for 1 hour. Add the remaining cup of water; stir and continue to simmer until the meat is fork-tender (approximately $3\frac{1}{2}$ hours).

Add 2–3 teaspoons of the curry and brown sugar; stir and continue to simmer.

Add the sweet potatoes and simmer until the potatoes are soft (not mushy). At this point, the sauce will be naturally thickened. Add salt if desired.

Serve over brown Basmati rice (allow approximately 45 minutes for the rice to cook prior to serving).

CALORIC CHART

246 Calories per Serving:	
27.343 g Protein	
19.572 g Carbohydrate	
6.230 g Total Fat:	1.319 g Saturated
	2.946 g Monounsaturated
	1.292 g Polyunsaturated
72.021 mg Cholesterol	
87.108 mg Sodium	
3.865 mg Iron	

INGREDIENTS

$1\frac{1}{2}$ tablespoons canola oil

2 bay leaves

2 cinnamon sticks

$\frac{1}{2}$ teaspoon cumin seed

6 whole black peppercorns

2 large Spanish onions, peeled and cut into $\frac{3}{4}$-inch pieces

4 garlic cloves, peeled and minced

2 teaspoons ginger root, peeled and minced

$\frac{1}{2}$ teaspoon turmeric

$\frac{1}{2}$ teaspoon ground cloves

2 cups of water

$1\frac{1}{2}$ pounds bison/buffalo stew meat, cut into chunks
   Dash of sea salt

3 carrots, peeled and cut into chunks

$\frac{1}{2}$ teaspoon ground ginger

$\frac{1}{2}$ cup *Laban (heavy strained yogurt)

$\frac{1}{4}$ cup $\frac{1}{2}$% milk

2–3 teaspoons (Madras) curry powder

1 tablespoon light brown sugar

2 large (4 cups) sweet potatoes (yellow, if possible), peeled and cut into 1-inch cubes

---
* See Ingredient Index

Opposite page:
Photo: Fred Ferris

FOUR ROASTED PEPPER, BEAN, AND SHREDDED BISON BURRITO GRANDE

Lime and garlic are predominant in this south-of-the-border treat. Serve with Spanish rice and ice-cold beer.   Yield: 6 servings

INGREDIENTS

FOR THE SHREDDED MEAT

2–3 pounds bison/buffalo brisket
3 garlic cloves, peeled
10 black peppercorns
Lime juice—enough to cover meat (for marinating)
1 large onion, peeled
2 dried whole small red chilies (Pico De Pajaro)
1½ tablespoons of light olive oil

FOR THE BEAN MIXTURE

2 cups *Anasazi beans
2 **dried** mulato chiles
3 **dried** New Mexico chiles
3 **fresh** Anaheim chiles
3 **fresh** jalapeño *chiles
3 garlic cloves, peeled
⅓ cup chopped fresh cilantro leaves
1 tablespoons *cranberry wine vinegar
6 tablespoons tomato paste
3 tablespoons lime juice (1½ limes)
2 teaspoons light olive oil
½ teaspoon sea salt
12 flat loaves of Lavash bread or flour tortillas (10½ inches)

＊ See Ingredient Index
＊＊ See Spices and Herbs

CALORIC CHART

520 Calories per Serving:
44.379 g Protein
59.362 g Carbohydrate
11.967 g Total Fat: 1.806 g Saturated
1.128 g Monounsaturated
0.385 g Polyunsaturated
93.917 mg Cholesterol
407.000 mg Sodium
9.073 mg Iron

DIRECTIONS

FOR THE MEAT

In a glass container, marinate the brisket with the garlic, peppercorns, and lime juice 12–24 hours in the refrigerator.

Place the bison brisket (without marinade) in a casserole. Retrieve the peppercorns and garlic from the marinade and add to the pot. Add enough water to cover the brisket completely, add the onion and dried red peppers. With the pot on the stove top, bring liquid to a boil. Reduce the heat so the mixture simmers. Continue simmering until the brisket is very tender (approximately 4 hours).

Remove from the heat and let the meat cool enough to handle. When the meat is cool, gently shred the meat with the tines of two forks. When all the meat is shredded, heat the oil in a large skillet until hot. Add the meat. Gently pan sauté the meat until glazed and browned. Remove the meat from the pan and set aside. While the meat is cooking, prepare the Anasazi beans.

FOR THE BEANS

Sort and wash the beans. Place the beans in a nonreactive pot. Quick cook (bring 8 cups of water and beans to a rapid boil, add more water if necessary to keep the beans covered). Turn off the heat and let the beans sit for 30 minutes. Return the beans to a light boil for 20 minutes or until the beans are tender. When the beans are cooked, drain and discard whatever liquid is left.

FOR THE PEPPERS

Roast the **dried** peppers (chiles) and garlic in a hot, dry skillet for several minutes (do not brown the peppers or they will taste bitter). *Do* brown the garlic.

Remove the dried peppers from the skillet. Remove the stems and seeds; discard. Place the peppers in a glass bowl and pour very **hot** water (just below the boiling point) over them and let them sit for 30 minutes. Remove the garlic from the skillet and set aside.

Roast the **fresh** peppers ＊＊ over a grill, gas flame (place a rack to hold peppers), or under the broiler until they are blistered and lightly blackened. Once the flesh of the peppers are blackened and blistered, place them in a glass bowl and cover with plastic wrap until the peppers are cool to the touch. Remove the stems and skin from each pepper. Gently open to remove and discard the seeds. (Do not rinse any of the peppers under water—it will reduce the impact of the flavor!)

DIRECTIONS

(CONTINUED)

▲▲▲▲▲▲▲▲▲

PUTTING IT TOGETHER

Remove the **dried** peppers from the water with a slotted spoon and place them in a food processor bowl. Add the roasted garlic, roasted peppers, cilantro leaves, vinegar, tomato paste, lime juice, olive oil, and salt to taste. Process, using the steel S blade, until smooth and paste-like.

Parfleche case. Tribe: Crow, circa 1880.
Courtesy of Richard Pohrt. Photo: Fred Ferris

Place the entire mixture in a glass bowl and add the very soft, cooked Anasazi beans and mix thoroughly (the blending will crush a portion of the beans). Adjust salt to taste.

In a skillet, lightly brown the tortillas or Lavash bread. Remove from the skillet. Place approximately ⅓ cup of the bean/pepper mixture and approximately 3 ounces of shredded meat in the center of the bread and fold both sides. Serve immediately.

99

BISON-HOISIN CREPE
WITH SHIITAKE MUSHROOMS

INGREDIENTS

FOR THE HOISIN SAUCE

8	garlic cloves, peeled and minced
2	green onions, ends cut and finely chopped
½	cup (light) black molasses
¼	cup light sodium-reduced soy sauce
5	tablespoons raspberry jam
¼	teaspoon dry Oriental hot mustard powder
4	tablespoons tomato paste
1	tablespoon canola oil
1–1½	teaspoons dried red chili flakes *or* Asian red pepper powder

FOR THE CREPES

1	cup pre-sifted flour
1¼	cups skim milk *or* 1¼ cups light beer
2	egg whites
	No-stick cooking spray

ADDITIONAL INGREDIENTS

2	ounces dried *shiitake mushrooms, reconstituted and thinly sliced
1½	pounds cooked bison/buffalo roast, thinly sliced (3 ounces per crepe)

---

*See Ingredient Index

Make these crepes with leftover roast. The strong and distinct taste of Hoisin paired with the delicacy of the crepe makes this dish unusual and intriguing.

Yield: 4 servings.

DIRECTIONS

FOR THE HOISIN SAUCE

(The sauce can be prepared earlier in the day or days ahead and placed in the refrigerator to keep fresh.)

Place garlic, onions, molasses, light soy sauce, jam, mustard powder, tomato paste, oil, and chili flakes in the bowl of a food processor. With a steel S blade, process until smooth.

FOR THE CREPES

Place the flour, skim milk (or beer), and egg whites in the bowl of a food processor. Process until smooth.

Spray a medium-sized skillet with no-stick cooking spray. Heat over medium heat. Add a ladle of batter and turn the pan quickly to coat the entire bottom.

When the cooking batter forms a "skin" on top, turn over and lightly brown. Remove the pan from the heat and remove the crepe.

Repeat the process (spraying the pan every third crepe) until all the batter is used.

PUTTING THE CREPES TOGETHER

Brush the surface of each crepe with the desired amount of Hoisin sauce. Place approximately 3 ounces of roast in the center of each crepe. Top the meat with the sliced mushrooms. Fold over each side of the crepe.

Serve warm with steamed Oriental vegetables.

CALORIC CHART

653 Calories per Serving:	
58.862 g Protein	
83.616 g Carbohydrate	
8.400 g Total Fat:	1.998 g Saturated
	3.781 g Monounsaturated
	1.693 g Polyunsaturated
141.000 mg Cholesterol	
588.000 mg Sodium	
14.776 mg Iron	

BISON BRISKET
WITH JUNIPER MARINADE

Wild and woodsy with the flavor of dried juniper. Slow-cooked brisket is tender and delicious served hot and great in sandwiches with grainy mustard or white horseradish sauce.

Yield: 4–6 servings (depending on the size of the brisket)

DIRECTIONS

Place the oil, wine vinegar, soy sauce, pepper powder, galangal, scallions, juniper berries, sugar, salt, cardamom, beef tea, allspice, and wine in the bowl of a food processor. Using the steel S blade, process until smooth. Place the bison brisket in a ceramic or glass container, pour the marinade over the meat and cover with plastic wrap.

Marinate the meat for 24 hours in the refrigerator.

When ready to cook, let the marinating roast come to room temperature. Preheat the oven to 275 degrees.

Lightly spray an ovenproof shallow pan with no-stick cooking spray. Place the brisket in the pan and pour the marinade over the meat.

Cover the pan with aluminium foil and bake 3–4 (or more) hours, until the meat is very tender. Remove from the oven, serve warm, with or without marinade.

INGREDIENTS

1	tablespoon canola oil
1	tablespoon *cranberry wine vinegar
2	tablespoons light sodium-reduced soy sauce
¼	teaspoon Asian red pepper powder
1	teaspoon ground galangal
1	cup scallions (white and green parts)
1	tablespoon crushed juniper berries
2	teaspoons sugar
	Dash of sea salt
1	teaspoon ground cardamom
½	teaspoon *beef tea
6	whole allspice
½	cup red wine
2–3	pounds bison/buffalo brisket
	No-stick cooking spray

* See Ingredient Index

CALORIC CHART

223 Calories per Serving:
33.586 g Protein
6.369 g Carbohydrate
5.176 g Total Fat:
    1.228 g Saturated
    2.428 g Monounsaturated
    0.966 g Polyunsaturated

93.917 mg Cholesterol
215.000 mg Sodium
4.988 mg Iron

BISON TENDERLOIN ROAST STUFFED WITH WILD RICE, CHESTNUTS, AND DRIED BLUEBERRIES

For an intimate evening with special friends, this tenderloin roast boasts an unusual and unique stuffing. Serve with additional stuffing on the side.

Yield: 4–6 servings

INGREDIENTS

FOR THE STUFFING

1   package (6-ounces) of *wild rice (prepared according to package directions), set aside the cooked rice.

1½   tablespoons light olive oil

1   medium onion (*Vidalia, if possible), peeled and chopped

3   garlic cloves, peeled and minced

1   cup chopped celery

1   can whole chestnuts (net weight drained 10-ounces/238 g) *or* (net weight drained 15.5-ounces/439 g)

3   ounces *dried blueberries

½   cup gourmet cooking sake (or any sweet wine)

1   tablespoon chopped fresh tarragon leaves
     Sea salt
     Peppercorn mélange, freshly ground

FOR THE MEAT

1½   pounds bison/buffalo tenderloin
     No-stick cooking spray
     Sea salt
     Peppercorn mélange, freshly ground

---

* See Ingredient Index

CALORIC CHART

635 Calories per Serving:	
47.186 g Protein	
81.193 g Carbohydrate	
9.968 g Total Fat:	2.150 g Saturated
	1.765 g Monounsaturated
	0.939 g Polyunsaturated
106.000 mg Cholesterol	
394.000 mg Sodium	
7.014 mg Iron	

DIRECTIONS

Prepare the stuffing first.

FOR THE STUFFING

Heat a skillet over high heat and add the oil. Add the onion and garlic. Cook over medium-high heat until browned. Add the celery and cook for approximately 6–8 minutes until the celery is slightly tender.

Drain the whole chestnuts and crumble them into the skillet. Mix thoroughly. Add the dried blueberries and sake or sweet wine. Stir until well mixed and the liquid is absorbed.

Add the cooked rice and chopped tarragon. Cook over low heat for 3–4 minutes. Add salt and peppercorn mélange to taste. (Makes 5 plus cups.)

Preheat the oven to 325 degrees.

Butterfly the bison tenderloin by cutting it horizontally through the midline, parallel to the meat surface (length and width), being careful not to puncture the other side of the tenderloin. Cut open larger to lay the tenderloin flat for easy stuffing or have your butcher butterfly the tenderloin for you.

Place a portion of the stuffing evenly across the flat surface (serve additional stuffing as a side dish). Roll the roast closed; tie with kitchen twine/string, making sure it is secure. Lightly spray the tied tenderloin with no-stick cooking spray; sprinkle with salt and ground peppercorn mélange.

Heat an indoor grill or skillet on the stove for several minutes. Place the roast on the grill just a few minutes on each side to lightly brown (it will sizzle). Remove the tenderloin roast from the grill or skillet and place it on a rack in a shallow pan designed for oven use.

Place the roast in a preheated oven. If the roast appears dry during the cooking process, remove it momentarily and spray lightly with cooking spray. Cook until the tenderloin roast reaches 135 degrees or the desired temperature (measure with a meat thermometer—an instant read thermometer is ideal for this). The tenderloin should not be cooked beyond medium-rare. When desired temperature is reached, remove the roast from the oven and let stand for 8–10 minutes before slicing. Remove the twine and slice 1½ inches thick.

Opposite page:
Photo: Fred Ferris

SLICED ROAST BISON PITA SANDWICHES WITH YOGURT SAUCE

Quick and easy best describes these tasty, herbed sandwiches made with left-over bison roast. Serve with a Mediterranean style salad...tabouli or minted-bean are excellent choices.   Yield: 8 sandwiches

INGREDIENTS

FOR THE SANDWICHES
- 2 tablespoons dried oregano
- ½ teaspoon dried thyme
- 1 teaspoon dried mint
- 4 large whole pita loaves (cut in half)
- 2 pounds cooked roast bison/buffalo, sliced and warmed
  - Onions, thinly sliced (desired amount)
  - Tomatoes, thinly sliced (desired amount)

FOR THE YOGURT SAUCE
- 1 pound (16-ounce container) *Laban (heavy strained yogurt)
- 2 tablespoons minced garlic (from a jar)
- ½ teaspoon sea salt
- ¼ cup thinly sliced cucumber, seeds removed before slicing

---

* See Ingredient Index

DIRECTIONS

FOR THE YOGURT SAUCE

Gently mix the Laban, garlic, salt, and cucumber with a rubber spatula until well mixed. Do not process in a food processor (keep yogurt thick).

FOR THE SANDWICHES

Mix the oregano, thyme, and mint together in a small container.

Open the pita bread pocket half and add 4 ounces of sliced (warmed) roast bison. Sprinkle with ⅛ of the mixed dried spices.

Add the desired amount of onions and tomatoes and top with a dollop of yogurt sauce. There will be additional sauce for those who prefer more.

CALORIC CHART

	255 Calories per Serving:	
36.806 g Protein		
16.611 g Carbohydrate		
3.748 g Total Fat:	1.423 g Saturated	
	1.247 g Monounsaturated	
	0.357 g Polyunsaturated	
95.676 mg Cholesterol		
335.000 mg Sodium		
4.708 mg Iron		

BLUE CORN POSOLE
BISON STEW

This interesting stew has a subtle hotness and gets its thick and chewy texture from the posole. Serve topped with chopped green onions and homemade corn bread croutons.   Yield: 6–8 servings

DIRECTIONS

Rinse the blue corn posole and soak it for 24 hours (in enough water to cover the blue corn). After soaking, rinse again and place in a large casserole with enough water to completely cover the posole. Add ½ teaspoon of salt and cook over medium heat for 2 hours. Turn off the heat and let posole remain in the water until ready for use.

Heat the olive oil over high heat in a large casserole. When the oil is hot, add the onion and minced garlic. Cook until transparent.

Add the meat and lightly brown. Remove any liquid and discard. Add the sliced jalapeños and mix well. Add the tomatoes (liquid included).

Drain the blue corn posole thoroughly and add it to the meat. Add the tomato paste, 6 ounces (½ bottle) of light beer and the cilantro, oregano, cayenne, and salt. Cover the casserole with a lid and cook on medium heat until the meat is tender (depending on what cut of meat you use, this could take from 1–3 hours).

During the cooking process, add the other 6 ounces of light beer and the lime juice. When the meat seems fork-tender, re-adjust spices and add any additional salt or Tabasco to taste.

INGREDIENTS

12	ounces *blue corn posole
½	teaspoon salt (for water)
1½	tablespoons light olive oil
1	medium Spanish onion, peeled and cut into ¾-inch pieces
3	garlic cloves, peeled and minced
2½	pounds bison/buffalo meat cut into small cubes
4	fresh jalapeño chilies, stems removed, seeded, and thinly sliced (wear rubber gloves!)
1	(28-ounce) can seasoned diced *tomatoes
3	tablespoons sun-dried tomato paste
1	bottle (12-ounce) of light beer
3	teaspoons dried cilantro
1	teaspoon dried oregano
1	teaspoon cayenne (or *Mombassa)
	Sea salt
	Juice of one fresh lime (1½–2 tablespoons)
	Tabasco *or* other hot sauce (optional)

_____

* See Ingredient Index

CALORIC CHART

288 Calories per Serving:

34.015 g Protein
24.351 g Carbohydrate
5.806 g Total Fat:

        1.445 g Saturated
        1.167 g Monounsaturated
        0.531 g Polyunsaturated

88.047 mg Cholesterol
330.000 mg Sodium
4.667 mg Iron

STEAK

RECIPES

STEAK AND VEGETABLE SANDWICHES WITH TANGY SAUCE

INGREDIENTS

FOR THE SANDWICHES
2 pounds (1¼-inch thick) bison/buffalo steaks
4 large green bell peppers, stems removed, seeded and sliced
4 large potatoes, peeled, boiled, and sliced
2 large onions (*Vidalia, if possible), peeled, and sliced
8 large slices of crusty Italian bread

FOR THE SAUCE
4 cups *tomato sauce
2 tablespoons Worcestershire sauce
1½ teaspoon dry Oriental hot mustard powder
4 tablespoons honey
2 tablespoons *jerk seasoning (*for recipe)
1 teaspoon garlic, peeled and minced
No-stick cooking spray

---

* See Ingredient Index

Open-faced and fabulous! We love to serve these "mile-high" sandwiches for brunches, picnics, tail-gate parties, or anytime. Serve with a dark green or spinach salad. Yield: 8 servings

DIRECTIONS

FOR THE TANGY SAUCE

In a medium saucepan, add the tomato sauce, Worcestershire sauce, mustard powder, honey, jerk seasoning, and garlic. Mix thoroughly. Bring to a boil and cook for 6 minutes. Set aside.

FOR THE SANDWICH FILLING

Spray a large skillet with no-stick cooking spray, heat over low until warm; add the onion and cook 8–10 minutes or until lightly tender. Add the green pepper and cooked potato slices. Cook for several minutes more until browned.

Spray steaks with the cooking spray. Add to warmed range grill (or skillet) and cook to desired doneness—turn frequently to evenly brown.

Remove the steaks from the heat and slice. Divide the steak and vegetable mixture into 8 equal portions. Place each portion over the slices of bread (open-face) and top with the warmed tangy sauce.

CALORIC CHART

378 Calories per Serving:	
31.603 g Protein	
54.706 g Carbohydrate	
2.384 g Total Fat:	0.830 g Saturated
	0.839 g Monounsaturated
	0.311 g Polyunsaturated
70.438 mg Cholesterol	
855.000 mg Sodium	
4.679 mg Iron	

BISON FILLETS
WITH ALMOND/SHALLOT SAUCE

The rich sauce that enhances the tender fillets makes this aristocratic entree extra special. Serve with herbed new potatoes and your favorite vegetable.

Yield: 6 servings

DIRECTIONS

FOR THE SAUCE

Heat the oil in a small saucepan. Add the shallots, garlic, and slivered almonds. Cook until the shallots are transparent. Stir in chicken tea, wine, water, peppercorn mélange, honey, and cilantro leaves. Bring to a boil and simmer for 6–8 minutes. Slowly add bread crumbs until sauce is at your desired consistency. Keep slightly warm.

FOR THE MEAT

Preheat the oven to 275 degrees.

Heat an empty skillet over high heat. Add the oil and heat to almost smoking. Add the steaks, turning them quickly from side to side to avoid burning. When the steaks are nicely browned (approximately 2 minutes), remove them from the heat.

Place the skillet with all the fillets into the oven and cook until the internal temperature reaches 135–145 degrees (medium-rare). An instant read thermometer is ideal for this. Remove the meat from the oven and serve with the almond/shallot sauce; garnish with artichoke hearts.

CALORIC CHART

389 Calories per Serving:	
32.244 g Protein	
22.099 g Carbohydrate	
15.001 g Total Fat:	2.098 g Saturated
	7.136 g Monounsaturated
	2.510 g Polyunsaturated
79.243 mg Cholesterol	
360.000 mg Sodium	
4.825 mg Iron	

INGREDIENTS

FOR THE SAUCE

1 tablespoon light olive oil
6 shallots, peeled and minced
2 large garlic cloves, peeled and minced
¾ cup slivered almonds
2½ tablespoons *chicken tea
1½ cups white wine
1½ cups water
¾ teaspoon ground peppercorn mélange
2 tablespoons honey
2 tablespoons chopped fresh cilantro leaves
  Herb seasoned stuffing mix processed into bread crumbs (as much as needed to thicken the sauce to desired consistency)

FOR THE MEAT

1 tablespoon canola oil
6 (4½ ounce) bison/buffalo tenderloin fillets

FOR THE GARNISH

  Canned artichoke hearts (4 or more per person), drained and quartered

---

* See Ingredient Index

STUFFED CHILLED ARTICHOKES
WITH CREAMY LEMON/LIME SAUCE

INGREDIENTS

FOR THE STUFFED ARTICHOKES

6	large artichokes
	Lemon juice for acidulated water
1	cup carrots, ends cut, peeled and cut into julienne
1	cup broccoli (flowers only, cut into small florets)
1	cup fresh *mushrooms (any exotic type), stems removed, washed and thinly sliced
1	cup rare to medium-rare grilled bison/buffalo steak cut into julienne

FOR THE LEMON/LIME SAUCE

1¼	cup *Laban (heavy strained yogurt)
2	tablespoons (canned) light evaporated milk
1½	tablespoons *chicken tea
3	tablespoons sweetened *lime juice
1½	tablespoons fresh lemon juice
3	teaspoons sugar
¼–½	teaspoon cayenne (or *Mombassa)

* See Ingredient Index

CALORIC CHART

> 247 Calories per Serving:
> 32.430 g Protein
> 24.576 g Carbohydrate
> 3.167 g Total Fat: 1.329 g Saturated
>   1.034 g Monounsaturated
>   0.379 g Polyunsaturated
> 73.567 mg Cholesterol
> 231.000 mg Sodium
> 4.930 mg Iron

Light and flavorful, guests are always hoping for seconds! Perfect for a luncheon or as a first course. The lemon/lime sauce is so tasty, you'll want to make extra for dipping the artichoke leaves.   Yield: 6 servings

DIRECTIONS

FOR COOKING THE ARTICHOKES/VEGETABLES

Remove the stem and bottom leaves from each artichoke. With a sharp knife, cut off the very top of the artichoke so that it is flat, and trim off any thorny tips.

Place the artichokes and lemon juice in a large casserole or stock pot. Add boiling water to completely cover the artichokes.

Over medium-high heat, cook the artichokes in a pot covered with a lid for 30–40 minutes or until the artichokes are tender and the bottom leaves pull off easily. Remove the artichokes from the pot and drain. Place them upside down on paper towels to drain any excess water.

While the artichokes are cooking, prepare the steamed vegetables.

In a medium-sized pot fitted with a stainless steel basket steamer, add the julienne carrots and cover the pot. Cook over medium-high heat for 5 minutes.

Add the broccoli florets and cook for an additional 3 minutes. Cook until the vegetables are crisp. Add the mushrooms to the pot and cook briefly.

Remove the steamed vegetables and drain. Place the cooked artichokes and cooked vegetables in the refrigerator to chill.

FOR THE LEMON/LIME SAUCE

Place the Laban, evaporated milk, chicken tea, lime juice, lemon juice, sugar, and cayenne pepper in a glass bowl. Whisk until smooth.

PUTTING THE ARTICHOKES TOGETHER

Remove the chilled artichokes from the refrigerator. Carefully pull open the artichokes and remove the "fuzzy" choke from each with a small spoon. Fill the cavities with the vegetables and bison mixed together. Re-shape the artichoke. Serve with lemon/lime sauce.

Opposite page: Buffalo Rawhide bag. Tribe: Crow, circa 1850.
Courtesy of Richard Pohrt. Photo: Fred Ferris

BARBECUED BISON KEBOBS WITH GINGER SOY

Interesting color. Interesting taste. Serve with steamed or fried rice and fresh sliced oranges or unusual Asian fruits.   Yield: 4 servings

INGREDIENTS

FOR THE GINGER MARINADE/SAUCE

2	large cloves of garlic, peeled and crushed
¼	cup canola oil
¼	cup light sodium-reduced soy sauce
1	tablespoon (light) black molasses
½	teaspoon dry Oriental hot mustard powder
4	slices (⅛ inch thick each) of ginger root, peeled and chopped
2	tablespoons cooking sake

FOR THE KEBOBS

4	bamboo skewer sticks, 10–12 inches long (soaked in water 12–24 hours)
1	pound eye of the round, tenderloin or any tender steak cut into 1½ inch thick cubes
24	large *cremini or button mushrooms, washed and stems removed
2	large red or yellow bell peppers, stems removed and seeded
2	large onions, peeled and each cut into 8 sections
	No-stick cooking spray

---

* See Ingredient Index

DIRECTIONS

FOR THE GINGER MARINADE/SAUCE

Combine the garlic, oil, light soy sauce, molasses, mustard powder, ginger root, and sake in the bowl of a food processor and process until smooth. Pour the mixture into a glass bowl and add the cubes of meat. Cover the bowl with plastic wrap and marinate in the refrigerator for 2 hours or more.

FOR THE KEBOBS

Remove the bison cubes from the marinade and pat dry with paper towels. Thread on skewers alternating with mushrooms, peppers, and onions—divide ingredients evenly between the 4 skewers. Lightly spray the entire skewer ingredients with cooking spray. Grill the kebobs (rare to medium).

While the meat and vegetables are grilling, in a small saucepan bring the remaining marinade to a boil. Use the heated marinade as a sauce for the kebobs.

CALORIC CHART

332 Calories per Serving:

27.178 g Protein
17.868 g Carbohydrate
16.105 g Total Fat:

    1.806 g Saturated
    8.842 g Monounsaturated
    4.393 g Polyunsaturated

70.438 mg Cholesterol
330.000 mg Sodium
3.997 mg Iron

BISON JERK STEAK
WITH SPICY YOGURT SAUCE

Island flavors dominate in this exciting entree. The yogurt is a cool contrast to the spicy heat of the jerk seasoning.   Yield: 4 servings

DIRECTIONS

FOR THE SPICY YOGURT SAUCE

Gently mix the Laban, Scotch bonnet pepper, garlic, and jerk seasoning in a bowl. Set aside.

FOR PREPARING THE MEAT

Preheat the oven to 275 degrees.

Place the dry jerk seasoning into a gallon-size "zipper" plastic bag. Lightly spray each steak with the cooking spray. Place one steak at a time into the bag and shake to cover with the seasoning.

Warm the skillet over high heat. Add the oil and heat to almost smoking. Add the steaks; turn several times to keep them from burning. Cook approximately 2 minutes; remove them from the heat.

Place the skillet with all the steaks into the oven and cook until the internal temperature reaches 135–145 degrees (medium-rare). An instant read thermometer is ideal for this.

Remove the meat from the oven and serve with the spicy yogurt sauce.

CALORIC CHART

INGREDIENTS

FOR THE SPICY YOGURT SAUCE

1 cup *Laban (heavy strained yogurt)
¼ Scotch bonnet pepper (or more, if desired), seeded and finely chopped (wear rubber gloves—hot!)
2 garlic cloves, peeled and minced
1 teaspoon *jerk seasoning (*for recipe)

FOR THE MEAT

6 tablespoons jerk seasoning (see above)
  No-stick cooking spray
4 (4 ounce) bison/buffalo rib eye steaks (1–1¼-inches thick)
1 tablespoon canola oil

---

* See Ingredient Index

216 Calories per Serving:	
27.849 g Protein	
10.539 g Carbohydrate	
6.637 g Total Fat:	1.650 g Saturated
	3.119 g Monounsaturated
	1.298 g Polyunsaturated
73.938 mg Cholesterol	
954.000 mg Sodium	
4.174 mg Iron	

GRILLED MEDALLIONS OF BUFFALO
WITH BOURBON PEACH CHUTNEY

INGREDIENTS

FOR THE MEAT AND MARINADE

½   cup light olive oil

2   garlic cloves, peeled and minced

1   tablespoon dried basil

½   tablespoon crushed bay leaf

   Juice of 1 small lemon (2–2½ tablespoons)

¼   teaspoon freshly ground black pepper

   Dash of sea salt

16   medallions (2 ounces each) of bison/buffalo

FOR THE BOURBON-PEACH CHUTNEY

   Makes 4 cups (freezes well)

1   (16-ounce) can sliced cling peaches in heavy syrup

½   cup bourbon

½   cup sugar

½   cup firmly packed light brown sugar

¼   teaspoon ground cloves

⅛   teaspoon ground cinnamon

½   tablespoon mustard seed

   Dash of sea salt

1   tablespoon crystallized ginger, thinly sliced

½   cup white vinegar

½   can (use 14 ounces of a 28 ounce can) seasoned diced *tomatoes, drained

1   large onion, peeled and thinly sliced

2   garlic cloves, peeled and minced

¼   cup dried cherries

½   fresh lemon, thinly sliced with peel and seeds removed

½   Scotch bonnet pepper, seeds removed and minced (wear rubber gloves—very hot!)

   Note: More pepper can be added to taste.

* See Ingredient Index

This refined, gourmet entree is perfect for a formal dinner or a special dining experience for the family. The recipe is not as complex as it seems and well worth the effort. Use leftover bourbon-peach chutney on just about anything.

Yield: 8 servings

DIRECTIONS

FOR THE MEAT AND MARINADE

Combine the olive oil, garlic, basil, bay leaf, lemon juice, black pepper, and salt in a food processor, process until smooth. Pour mixture into a glass bowl; add the medallions, cover with plastic wrap, and marinate in the refrigerator for 4 hours or more.

FOR THE BOURBON-PEACH CHUTNEY

Drain the peaches and reserve 1 cup of the syrup.

Using a casserole dish or heavy saucepan, add the peach syrup (set peaches aside until later), bourbon, both sugars, cloves, cinnamon, mustard seed, salt, ginger, vinegar, tomatoes, onions, garlic, dried cherries, lemon slices, and Scotch bonnet pepper.

Stirring frequently, cook over high heat bringing the mixture to a boil (do not leave unattended). Continue to boil for 20–30 minutes or until the mixture appears thick and liquid is reduced.

Add the peaches and return to a boil. Continue to cook for 3–5 minutes; don't let the peaches break apart (use a rubber spatula). Set aside. (You may serve the chutney warm or cool.)

Remove the medallions of buffalo from the marinade. Grill (rare or medium-rare). When the steak is removed from the grill, top with the cooled or warm bourbon-peach chutney. Serve.

CALORIC CHART

382 Calories per Serving:	
26.068 g Protein	
50.000 g Carbohydrate	
6.011 g Total Fat:	1.340 g Saturated
	0.994 g Monounsaturated
	0.325 g Polyunsaturated
70.438 mg Cholesterol	
203.000 mg Sodium	
4.374 mg Iron	

Opposite page:
Photo: Fred Ferris

BISON SPINACH BALLOTTINE IN TOMATO-COGNAC SAUCE

▲▲▲▲▲▲▲▲▲▲◆▲▲▲▲▲▲▲▲▲▲

INGREDIENTS

▲▲▲▲▲▲▲▲▲

¼ cup dried oyster or any exotic dried *mushrooms, reconstituted *or* 8–10 firm, whole button mushrooms

½ *or* 1 cup boiling water (½ cup if using fresh mushrooms, 1 cup if using reconstituted mushrooms)

½ cup freshly grated Parmesan cheese

3 garlic cloves, peeled and minced

1 bunch chopped curly parsley, stems removed

½ cup pine nuts, chopped

1½ pounds bison/buffalo top round steak, partially frozen (sliced to ⅛ inch thickness)

1 bunch of fresh spinach, stems removed and leaves washed thoroughly

2 tablespoons light olive oil

2½ tablespoons cognac

2 tablespoons *sun-dried tomato paste

2 teaspoons *beef tea

1 whole bay leaf

¼ teaspoon dried sweet basil

¼ teaspoon dried oregano

⅛ teaspoon powdered sage
Dash of sea salt
Dash of freshly ground peppercorn mélange

½ cup medium-dry red wine

1 tablespoon pre-sifted flour

---
* See Ingredient Index

Rolled with spinach, Parmesan, and pinenuts, these "roll-ups" are simple yet very elegant and make for an artistic presentation. Serve with oven-roasted parsleyed potatoes and mixed baby greens.   Yield: 6 servings

DIRECTIONS

▲▲▲▲▲▲▲▲▲

In a glass bowl, soften the mushrooms in boiling water.

In a separate bowl, mix the Parmesan cheese, garlic, parsley, and pine nuts.

Spread the cheese/nut mixture evenly over each slice of bison meat and top with fresh spinach leaves. Roll the meat up (like a jelly-roll) and tie securely with kitchen twine.

Heat the olive oil in a large skillet over medium-high heat. Add the bison rolls and brown on all sides turning them frequently to prevent sticking.

In a small saucepan heat the cognac. Pour over the meat rolls and ignite. Remove the meat rolls from the skillet and set aside.

To the same skillet, add the softened mushrooms and water. Add the sun-dried tomato paste, beef tea, bay leaf, basil, oregano, sage. Add salt and peppercorn mélange to taste.

In a small glass container, whisk together the wine and the flour until smooth. Add to the skillet and continue to cook until the sauce is thickened, stirring constantly.

Reduce the heat to medium-low and add the meat ballentines to the skillet. Cover with a lid and simmer for a few minutes until the meat is tender. Do not overcook. Serve with the sauce.

CALORIC CHART

▲▲▲▲▲▲▲▲▲▲

320 Calories per Serving:	
32.280 g Protein	
7.324 g Carbohydrate	
15.271 g Total Fat:	3.971 g Saturated
	4.188 g Monounsaturated
	2.354 g Polyunsaturated
77.021 mg Cholesterol	
287.000 mg Sodium	
4.809 mg Iron	

BISON KEBOBS
WITH PEANUT SAUCE

Bison kebobs with peanut sauce is great for entertaining...everything can be prepared ahead of time. And the cook is not left in the kitchen the entire evening! Serve with a bowl of sweet rice and a side dish of sautéed mushrooms and bean sprouts. The peanut sauce is delicious as a dip for fresh raw vegetables.   Yield: 6 servings

DIRECTIONS

FOR THE PEANUT SAUCE

Spray a medium saucepan with cooking spray. Sauté the onions and garlic over medium-high heat until transparent. Add the chile peppers and continue to sauté for 3 more minutes. Add the soy sauce, brown sugar, anchovy paste, cumin, coriander, and cardamom. Stir until well blended.

Lower the heat or use a defuser before adding the coconut milk. Add the peanut butter and continue to cook over very low heat for 1 hour and 15 minutes, stirring occasionally.

When mixture appears thick and darkened, remove from the heat and whisk in ½% milk to desired thickness. Serve the sauce at room temperature.

FOR THE BISON KEBOBS AND MARINADE

In a glass container, add the ginger root, garlic, light soy sauce, green onion, sake, and brown sugar. Pour the marinade over the meat and marinate for 45 minutes or more.

Remove the meat from the marinade and pat dry with paper towels. Thread meat on pre-soaked skewers. Lightly spray the entire skewer meat with cooking spray.

Grill the meat kebobs to desired doneness. Serve with the peanut sauce.

CALORIC CHART

	430 Calories per Serving:	
36.626 g Protein		
18.030 g Carbohydrate		
24.510 g Total Fat:	5.426 g Saturated	
	10.970 g Monounsaturated	
	6.413 g Polyunsaturated	
72.193 mg Cholesterol		
379.000 mg Sodium		
4.357 mg Iron		

INGREDIENTS

6   bamboo skewers, 10–12 inches long (soaked in water 12–24 hours)

FOR THE PEANUT SAUCE

No-stick cooking spray
1   medium onion, peeled and finely chopped
2   garlic cloves, peeled and minced
2   fresh hot green chile peppers, seeds removed and minced (wear rubber gloves—very hot!) (more can be added—adjust to taste)
½   teaspoon light sodium-reduced soy sauce
2   teaspoons light brown sugar
1   teaspoon anchovy paste
1   teaspoon ground cumin
1   teaspoon coriander
1   teaspoon ground cardamom
⅓   cup light coconut milk
1   cup creamy peanut butter
    ½% milk (use as much as is desired to thin out the paste)

FOR THE BISON KEBOBS AND MARINADE

1½   pounds eye of the round, tenderloin, *or* any tender steak, cut into 1-inch cubes
¼   inch slice of ginger root, peeled and minced
2   garlic cloves, peeled and minced
1½   tablespoons light sodium-reduced soy sauce
1   finely chopped green onion
1½   tablespoons sake
1   tablespoon light brown sugar
    No-stick cooking spray

BRASH BISON BORSCHT

▲▲▲▲▲▲▲▲▲▲◆▲▲▲▲▲▲▲▲▲▲

INGREDIENTS

▲▲▲▲▲▲▲▲▲

- 1 pound (3–5) parsnips, ends removed, peeled, and chopped
- 2 carrots, ends removed, peeled, and chopped
- 1 (28-ounce) can seasoned diced *tomatoes, with liquid
- 16 whole cloves
- 1 large Spanish onion, peeled only—cloves spiked into onion
- 1 tablespoon sugar
- 1 teaspoon sea salt
- 1½ pounds bison/buffalo stew meat
- 1 tablespoon *beef tea
- 1 pound raw fresh beets, peeled, and shredded
- 2 bay leaves
- 6 cups of green cabbage, cut into ¾-inch pieces
- 1 tablespoon raspberry wine vinegar
- ½ teaspoon freshly ground black pepper
- ½ teaspoon–½ tablespoon Asian red pepper powder
- 4 tablespoons tomato paste
- 4 tablespoons light brown sugar

---

* See Ingredient Index

This sweet, hot, and spicy soup is a combination of Russian borscht and Korean kim-chee. Serve it hot or cold...anytime.   Yield: 6–8 servings

DIRECTIONS

▲▲▲▲▲▲▲▲

Place the parsnips, carrots, diced tomatoes, onion spiked with cloves, sugar, salt, stew meat, and beef tea in a large casserole. Add enough water to cover and bring to a boil. Cover with a lid and simmer 2½–3 hours or until meat is fork-tender.

Add the beets, bay leaves, cabbage, vinegar, fresh black pepper, red pepper powder, tomato paste, and light brown sugar.

Simmer approximately 1½ hours longer or until cabbage and beets are tender. Stir the borscht periodically. Serve hot!

CALORIC CHART

▲▲▲▲▲▲▲▲▲▲

221 Calories per Serving:	
21.763 g Protein	
30.008 g Carbohydrate	
2.025 g Total Fat:	0.663 g Saturated
	0.701 g Monounsaturated
	0.291 g Polyunsaturated
52.828 mg Cholesterol	
546.000 mg Sodium	
4.060 mg Iron	

APPENDIXES

SPICES AND HERBS

ALLSPICE

A clovelike taste, this brownish red spice adds a pungent, sweet peppery flavor to any recipe. Allspice comes from the Jamaica pepper tree and is also called Jamaica pepper. The berries are gathered prior to ripening, then dried to maintain their most aromatic potency. Allspice comes whole or ground into powder.

Ground Syrian allspice is a combination of allspice and other spices creating a very hot, intense seasoning, terrific with meats, rices, and sauces. See the Ingredient Index for my recipe for Syrian Allspice.

ASIAN RED PEPPER

(See CHILES—Specific Chiles)

BASIL(S)

Basil is a fragrant, leafy plant grown easily in gardens and window boxes. A member of the mint family, this full-flavored herb has many varieties.

Sweet Basil—green leafed with a mild, sweet, but peppery flavor and a hint of cloves and mint. Sweet basil is usually associated with pesto sauces and meats.

Opal Basil—purple-leafed basil is ornamental and tart. This basil differs from the common variety by having a deeper flavor and no trace of mint. Opal basil is usually associated with vinegars but is a delicious addition to spaghetti sauces and savory dishes.

BAY LEAVES

Bay leaves come from an aromatic, evergreen, shrublike tree. The leaves appear leathery and dark green and are commonly sold dried (usually whole). The leaves have a strong, herbaceous flavor and are usually used sparingly in culinary endeavors—from marinades to stews. French cooking includes this herb as an integral ingredient of the *bouquet garni*. The bay leaf is used not only with food but for medicinal purposes, cosmetics, and ornamentation.

CARDAMOM

Cardamom comes from the perennial cardamom plant. The aromatic pods are used whole, seeds only, or ground seeds (powder) depending upon the recipe. Whole pods are used to flavor teas and coffee. The flavor is similar to that of ginger with the added taste of pine, and can be interchanged with ginger if there is a need. This spice, used in sweet or savory dishes, is common in Middle Eastern cookery and has a history that traces back thousands of years. Cardamom is also used in Scandinavian and Indian cuisines. Cardamom is generally more expensive than other spices, but worth it!

CAYENNE PEPPER

(See CHILES—Specific chiles)

CHILES (Capsicum)

Chiles (varieties of peppers) come from annual or perennial plants that are quite shrublike. Chiles themselves are the nonaromatic pods of these plants and can pack a lot of heat! Generally, the smaller the pepper, the hotter the taste, as the capsaicin present in the seeds are closer to the flesh of the small pod.

The heat of peppers is rated on a temperature scale from 1–10, least heat to hottest. Another scale (known as Scoville Units) rates from 0–300,000 units.

Wear rubber or surgical gloves (easily obtained at any pharmacy) for seeding and deveining hot chiles to avoid any distress related to touching eyes or face. Heat remains a long time on hands, fingers, and fingernails that have handled capsaicin.

Utilizing fresh or dry chiles is an interesting means of creating unique flavors in foods. The combination of both dry and fresh chiles together creates intricate complexities of these flavors.

There are over 150 varieties of chiles. Many are easily obtained at grocery and specialty stores. Some unusual varieties may have to be cultivated in your own garden. See the Ingredient Index for sources.

Chiles have been used in many forms for centuries for both medicinal and culinary purposes. Hot chiles aid in digestion and are utilized medicinally for stomach ailments; they have also been used as decongestants. The present day culinary popularity of chiles have made them far more available for consumers than ever before.

SPECIFIC CHILES USED IN RECIPES:

Anaheim—heat 2–3 / 500–1,500 Scoville units.

This long, green pepper may be pale to bright in color and is approximately 6-inches long and 2-plus-inches wide. The heat varies, as with all chiles, depending on where they have been cultivated. This chile can be interchanged with the hot finger peppers in all recipes. These chiles are generally found fresh and are readily available year round.

Asian Red Pepper—powder

Fiery-hot ground red Asian chilies; use sparingly—this is "beyond the beyond."

Cayenne—(Cayenne Pepper) heat 7–8 / 30,000–50,000 Scoville units.

Cayenne pepper comes from the cayenne pepper plant; the small ripened fruit is usually dried and ground. Its primary use is to season food or be used as an ingredient in hot sauces. This distinctively pungent and incredibly hot herb is not a relative to black pepper, but used in a similar manner—adding "bite" to whatever it is added to.

Paprika is the mildest form of cayenne. Cayenne chiles (fresh) can easily be used in recipes requiring hot peppers.

Chili Powder—heat 1–2.

Chili powder is a mixture of ground, dry chile peppers with additional spices and herbs.

Hot Green Finger Chiles—heat 2–4 / 1,000–1,500 Scoville units.

These smooth, thin, dark green chiles are approximately 5 inches long and ½–¾-inches wide.

Jalapeño—heat 5–6 / 2,500–5,000 Scoville units.

Jalapeños are bright to dark green, relatively small chiles generally associated with Mexican cuisine. They are a versatile pepper that can be added to almost any food. These chiles are readily available in many forms: fresh, pickled, canned, and bottled.

Mombassa—ground red pepper powder (80,000 Scoville units).

Fiery hot. Used in place of cayenne for a hotter pepper flavor.

Mulato—heat 2–4 / 1,000–1,500 Scoville units.

Mulato chiles are a type of dried poblano chile. This long, dark brown chile has a smoky tobacco taste with the subtlety of licorice and cherry. The mulato chile is a strong component when added with fresh chiles to create intricate flavors. Mulato chiles can be found dried in specialty food shops.

New Mexico (Nu Mex Eclipse)—heat 2–3 / 500–1,000 Scoville units.

The New Mexico eclipse is comparable in taste and appearance to the New Mexico red, but is deep brown in color. This dry chile mixes well combined with other dry peppers or in combination with other fresh and dried chiles.

New Mexico Red—heat 2–3 / 500–1,000 Scoville units.

New Mexico reds are long, bright red chiles approximately 6-inches long and 2-inches wide. This chile has a crisp-heat quality and is generally sold dried and crushed for use on pizzas, in stews, sauces, and soups.

Scotch Bonnet—heat 9–10 / 100,000–300,000 Scoville units.

The Scotch bonnet chile is incredibly hot; this family member to the habanero chile can easily be interchanged for recipes. These small rounded chiles come in a variety of colors: red, yellow, orange, and green—all equally hot and fruity, with traces of smoky flavoring. Scotch bonnets are naturals with chutneys, sauces, and fruited curries.

CHILI POWDER

(See CHILES—Specific Chiles)

CHINESE 5 SPICE(S)

Chinese 5 spice(s) is an aromatic blend of spices generally including: cinnamon, star anise, fennel, cloves, ginger, licorice, Szechuan peppercorns, and white peppercorn. Star anise dominates this flavorful mixture. This spice is usually associated with Asian cuisine and should be used sparingly.

CILANTRO

Cilantro are the green leaves of the coriander plant. Resembling flat-leaf parsley, cilantro is sometimes referred to as Chinese or Mexican parsley. However, the flavor of this distinctive, flat-leafed plant is not at all parsleylike. Cilantro can be purchased fresh or dried. The fresh leaf has a more intense and unique flavor.

CINNAMON

Cinnamon comes from the shoots (or quills, the inner bark) of the cinnamon tree. This pungent-flavored herb is used in bark-form (cinnamon stick) or ground, depending on the specific recipe. The taste is clovelike and somewhat sweet, enabling it to enhance an enormous range of foods. Cinnamon is aromatic and can be used in beverages or for decorative purposes, especially at holiday times.

CLOVES

Cloves are the flower buds of the clove tree. They are strongly aromatic and distinctive. The brownish red flowerlike buds are used whole or ground. This spice works well with fruit recipes of all types, beverages, and other sweet and/or savory foods.

CORIANDER

Coriander is an aromatic, spherical seed that has been used for culinary purposes for 3,000 years. This seed can be utilized whole or ground. Typically used in Middle Eastern and Indian dishes, this spice is mildly spicy-sweet with a slight orange taste. It is commonly used whole, as a pickling-spice, and ground, in other recipes containing meat, rice, and vegetables. The leaves (cilantro) are used in many recipes and have their own distinctive taste.

(Also see CILANTRO)

CUMIN

Cumin are the seeds of a European grown spice shrub; deep, quick, and hot in flavor, cumin is used either in seed or powdered form. Typically used in Indian, Middle Eastern, and Mexican recipes, this pungent spice has a lasting quality that is terrific in meats, soups, chilies, and stews.

CURRY POWDER

Curry powder is a mixture of spices generally incorporating: red chiles, coriander, cumin, mustard seeds, peppercorns, fenugreek, ginger, turmeric, and curry leaves. Curry powder is commonly used in Indian and Caribbean cuisines or in any dish requiring a distinctive, hot flavor.

ELEPHANT GARLIC

Elephant garlic is a member of the onion family. Usually ranges from about 3–5 inches in diameter. Its appearance is similar to that of an overgrown bulb of garlic. These large bulbs are milder than regular garlic cloves, making them a nice addition to recipes that require subtle flavor.

FENUGREEK

Fenugreek is a fragrant, annual herb that appears cloverlike and has medicinal, culinary, and practical fodder usage. It has a nutty, bitter celery flavor with a faint taste of maple. Fenugreek is available in whole seed, crushed seed, and powdered form. The leaves are used for culinary purposes. This versatile spice is used in Middle Eastern and Indian cuisines—in everything from halvah to curry.

GALANGAL

Galangal is the root of the galangal plant and a member of the ginger family. This aromatic root has a slight peppery taste and is generally sold as powder or in dried sliced pieces. Galangal's seemingly Far Eastern taste has been used in Egypt and Arabia for over a thousand years for both culinary and medicinal purposes.

GARLIC

Garlic is a member of the onion family. It grows as a bulb consisting of numerous cloves and covered in a paper-thin skin. Garlic comes in many forms: fresh (in bulbs), powdered, juice, and minced in jars.

This distinct and flavorful herb is utilized in numerous ways and in a multitude of recipes. Roast garlic by lightly oiling the papery skin and baking in a hot oven (400 degrees F.) for one half-hour; while still warm, spread softened cloves on bread as a no-fat replacement for butter or margarine. Garlic has been touted, not only for its culinary appeal, but also for its medicinal attributes. Easy peeling of a clove is done by pressing it gently with the palm of your hand on the flat side of a large knife, allowing the papery covering to slip off.

(Also see ELEPHANT GARLIC)

GINGER

Ginger appears in various forms; this root can be found either dried, powdered, crystalized, or fresh in lump form. It is pungent with a slight citrus flavor. This Asian staple spice is primarily used fresh (peeled), dried, or ground into a powder. Ginger is aromatic and distinctive, often utilized with cloves, nutmeg, and cinnamon.

HORSERADISH

Horseradish is the root of the horseradish plant, a relative of the mustard family. Once used primarily as a medicinal herb, ground or grated horseradish adds a pungent, hot mustard taste to many recipes. Powdered horseradish is mild in comparison to the freshly grated root.

JERK SEASONING

Jerk seasoning is a combination of spices that, when mixed, are sweet, spicy-hot, and complex. This seasoning has a taste familiar to the foods of the Caribbean. Although the "jerk" sensation has arrived here in the United States, pre-made is still not always easy to find. Some grocery stores and specialty gourmet shops carry it. I have developed my own version (recipe) after tasting a small portion of jerk seasoning sprinkled on a fruit salad seven years ago in Florida.

(See the Ingredient Index for the recipe to make Jerk Seasoning.)

JUNIPER

Juniper are berries from a dwarf, prickly leafed evergreen. These peppercorn-sized berries take two years to fully ripen. Generally, when one thinks of juniper berries, it is more associated with gin or the French beer called Genievre, than with food. Juniper berries are delicious when used in marinades and sauces specifically for meat or wild game. Whole berries can be used when poaching foods or in the

brewing of tea. The flavor of these dark berries is strong; use sparingly.

LEMON GRASS

Lemon grass is an Asian grass with a bulbous base. It is used in many Asian recipes. It can be purchased fresh, dried in strips, or powdered. The flavor of fresh lemon grass is lemonlike; the dried is less flavorful. Its scent is comparable to that of the lemon verbena plant. Lemon grass is a delightful accent to sauces and stir-frys.

MACE

(See NUTMEG)

MINT

Garden mint comes from the leaves of the mint plant—this perennial herb of character has a long list of family members and a history that includes racy myths, legends, and old wives tales. These aromatic plants grow easily and are quite intrusive. When growing more than one variety, it is important to keep each type separate or they will crossbreed, changing their original flavors. The green, aromatic leaves can be used fresh, frozen, or dried in food, drinks, teas, and can be used medicinally. Mint has a pleasantly pungent, spicy, fresh taste, and is widely used in American, English, and ethnic cuisine.

MUGWORT

Mugwort is a perennial, wild herb that grows 5–6 feet in height and appears dark green on top and wooly white underneath. This plant spreads easily and grows virtually anywhere, from deserts to roadsides. Having a slightly bitter taste, this soft powdered spice has a questionable history with questionable usage. If used in food, it should be used in very small amounts. Asian people use it primarily as "coloring" for doughs. Many people still associate mugwort as an ingredient in herbal baths, to relieve aches and pains, or, to keep away moths.

Native Americans used mustard in different forms. The green spring leaves and seeds were eaten. A fine powder of black mustard seed mixed with animal fats were used for a poultice on sprains and sore joints.

MUSTARD SEEDS

Mustard seeds come from hardy, annual, mustard plants (white, brown, and black) that grow easily and in many countries throughout the world. Mustard has been a culinary staple for thousands of years. Black mustard seeds are the strongest and most pungent, and white are the mildest. These flavorful seeds are virtually nonaromatic. Mustard seeds can be used whole, ground, or blended. Oriental hot mustard powder is the "hot" version of traditional mustard powder; it is mixed with water to form a paste and served as a condiment.

NUTMEG

The nutmeg kernel comes from the nutmeg tree. Mace is the thin, lacelike membrane of the shell. Both mace and nutmeg are similar in their aromas as well as taste, with nutmeg being slightly sweeter. Nutmeg can be purchased whole or ground. Freshly grated nutmeg is considerably stronger in flavor to that of the ground. It may be used in a variety of sweet or savory dishes, in good combination with cardamom, ginger, cinnamon, and cloves.

OREGANO

Oregano is closely associated with wild marjoram and is an aromatic, green, bushy perennial. This distinct peppery-flavored herb is generally associated with Italian cuisine and commonly teamed up with thyme in a variety of recipes. Oregano is easily cultivated in most climates and can be purchased fresh, dried, or powdered.

ORIENTAL HOT MUSTARD POWDER

(See MUSTARD SEEDS)

PAPRIKA

(See CHILES—Cayenne)

PARSLEY

Parsley is a biennial plant that grows easily. This dark green, leafy plant comes in several varieties: curly leaf, flat leaf, and Hamburg (parsnip rooted). Parsley is versatile as a culinary ingredient. High in vitamins, decorative, and easily blended with many foods, parsley remains a staple in most kitchens. Parsley is sold fresh or chopped and dried.

PEPPERCORN MÉLANGE

Peppercorn mélange is a combination of green, white, pink, and black peppercorns. The combination of peppercorns provides a slightly different taste to that of just one type of peppercorn—all pungent, with some slightly hotter than others. The multicolors are quite attractive, and can always be interchanged with black pepper.

PICKLING SPICE

Pickling spice is a combination of spices used together to infuse flavor in pickling meat, fruits, or vegetables, flavoring vinegars, or preparing chutneys, marinades, and sauces. Pickling spice may be added whole or infused (utilizing a tea strainer or muslin bag to hold the loose spices). Pickling spice is comprised of whole allspice, mustard seeds, whole cloves, coriander seeds, whole black and white peppercorns, crushed bay leaves, cardamom pods or seeds, dill seeds, dried ginger, mace, slivered cinnamon bark (or broken cinnamon quills), and dried red or chile peppers. Although pickling spice is easily obtainable at any grocery store, with the ingredients on hand, you may wish to make it yourself. Bottled, it makes a nice gift.

(See the Ingredient Index for my recipe for Pickling Spice.)

ROSEBUD POWDER

Powdered rosebud leaves are used mostly in potpourris and in some Syrian allspice recipes.

SAGE

Sage is a fragrant perennial subshrub having numerous varieties. Culinary sage has a musty, pungent, lemon flavor with a slight taste of camphor. It is greyish green with textured oblong leaves. Sage is indigenous to the Mediterranean; specifically, the northern coastal area, although it is grown in many other countries. Sage is frequently associated with stuffing and savory dishes and, like mugwort, seems to be linked with neutralizing fatty meats and fowl. For thousands of years sage was

Native Americans mixed sage and bear grease together for curing skin sores. Sage leaves were also used as infusions for medicinal baths and cleansing of their teeth.

considered primarily a medicinal herb. Today it has earned respect in the areas of cooking, cosmetics, and ornamentation. Sage can occasionally be purchased fresh. It is easily obtained dried.

SEA SALT

Sea salt is a mineral used as a spice. Evaporation of seawater is the earliest method of obtaining salt. Most salt produced by this method is 95–98 percent pure sodium chloride.

SCOTCH BONNET PEPPER

(See CHILES—Specific Chiles)

SHALLOTS

Shallots are a member of the onion family. These small bulbous onions with brown-orange skins have a subtle onion flavor, excellent in sauces and marinades.

SUMAC

Sumac are the deep colored, dried berries of the sumac bush. These berries can be used whole or ground and are typically included in many Middle Eastern dishes. This spice has practically no aroma, just a somewhat sour taste that remains fruity and interesting to the food it accompanies.

TARRAGON

Tarragon is an aromatic, lanky, green perennial common to France and Russia. The French tarragon has a delicate, aniselike quality. Russian tarragon is somewhat bitter in taste. Both of these tarragons can be purchased fresh or dried. Its usage is primarily culinary; use in small quantities.

THYME

Thyme is an aromatic, small branchy perennial shrub having many species and flavors. This versatile herb has medicinal and culinary properties. Sprigs are used in flavoring vinegars, meats, and soups. The leaves which are most commonly used work well with all types of foods (meats and vegetables alike). Fresh or dry, thyme's gentle flavor allows it to blend well with other spices.

TURMERIC

Turmeric is related to the ginger root. Fresh, the turmeric root is quite orange in color; dry, it appears to be more orange-yellow. The deeper the color, the higher the quality of the spice. Mostly used in Indian and Asian food, it is a contributing spice to curry powder. Turmeric, vibrant in color, has a slightly bitter and musky flavor. It is used in dyes and the coloring of prepared mustards and sauces.

Sea salt can be easily interchanged with ground, coarse Kosher salt in any recipe.

INGREDIENT

INDEX

ALLSPICE

(See SYRIAN ALLSPICE—includes Recipe)

ANASAZI BEANS

Anasazi beans are grown organically at high altitudes. They are an attractive bean resembling a pinto pony, full flavored, and mildly sweet in taste. These beans cook faster and are milder than the familiar pinto bean. Anasazi beans can be purchased from specialty shops or shipped directly from:

Adobe Milling Co., Inc.
P. O. Box 596
09006 E. Highway 666
Dove Creek, CO 81324
1-800-54-ADOBE
1-303-677-2667 FAX

BASMATI RICE

A brown or white rice that is full flavored, firm in consistency, and has a nutty flavor. This rice has grown for centuries in northern India near the foothills of the Himalayas. Basmati rice can be purchased from most groceries, Asian markets, or gourmet food shops.

BEANS

(See ANASAZI BEANS)

BEEF TEA

Natural flavored beef concentrate—bouillon. Original Smithers Gourmet English

Beef Tea is fat free, low in calories, and caffeine free—can be purchased at some grocery stores, gourmet food shops, or shipped directly from:

    Milani Foods
    Alberto-Culver USA, Inc.
    2525 Armitage Avenue
    Melrose Park, IL 60160
       1-708-450-3000

BLUE CORN POSOLE

Natural blue corn kernels, blue corn posole can be purchased at gourmet food and specialty shops or directly from:

    Los Chileros de Nuevo Mexico
    P. O. Box 6215
    Santa Fe, NM 87502
       1-505-471-6967

BLUEBERRIES

(See DRIED CRANBERRIES, BLUEBERRIES, AND CHERRIES)

BOUILLON

(See BEEF TEA)
(See CHICKEN TEA)

CHERRIES

(See DRIED CRANBERRIES, BLUEBERRIES, AND CHERRIES)

CHICKEN TEA

Chicken base—bouillon, Original Smithers Gourmet Chicken Tea is fat free and low in calories—can be purchased at some grocery stores, gourmet food shops, or shipped directly from:

    Milani Foods
    Alberto-Culver USA, Inc.
    2525 Armitage Avenue
    Melrose Park, IL 60160
       1-708-450-3000

CHILES

(See PEPPERS—Roasting Instructions)
(See PEPPERS—Seeds for Planting (for more detail see Chiles in the Spices and Herbs Appendix))

COCONUT MILK, LITE

Coconut milk that contains 75 percent less fat and 66 percent fewer calories than regular coconut milk. Light/lite coconut milk can be purchased in many grocery stores and stores that specialize in Asian products.

COOKWARE, ENAMELED CAST IRON

(See LE CREUSET)

COOKWARE, KITCHEN NEEDS

(See KITCHEN GLAMOR)
(See WILLIAMS-SONOMA)

CORN, BLUE

(See BLUE CORN POSOLE)

CRANBERRIES

(See DRIED CRANBERRIES, BLUEBERRIES, AND CHERRIES)

CRANBERRY WINE VINEGAR

Cranberry wine vinegar is a light, mild, cranberry-flavored wine vinegar. Chatham Winery's Cranberry Wine Vinegar comes in a fabulous, clear, lobster-shaped bottle, and can be purchased from specialty gourmet food shops or shipped directly from:

Chatham Winery
Route 28, The Cornfield
Chatham, MA 02633
1-508-945-0300

CREMINI MUSHROOMS

(See MUSHROOMS—Unusual)

DAIKON RADISH

A large, white Asian vegetable with a delightful radish taste. Daikon radishes can be purchased at some grocery stores, specialty fruit and vegetable stores, or at Asian markets.

DEI FRATELLI TOMATO SAUCE/ DEI FRATELLI SEASONED DICED TOMATOES

Terrific tomato products in a can with a white lining. Dei Fratelli tomato products can be purchased in some grocery stores or shipped directly from:

Hirzel Canning Co.
411 Lemoyne Road
Northwood, OH 43619
1-800-837-1631

DRIED CRANBERRIES, BLUEBERRIES AND CHERRIES

Delicious dried fruits. Dried fruits can be purchased at some grocery stores, gourmet food shops, or shipped directly from:

American Spoon Foods, Inc.
P. O. Box 566
Petoskey, MI 49770
1-800-222-5886

DRIED MUSHROOMS

(See MUSHROOMS—Unusual)

DRIED TOMATO PRODUCTS

(See SONOMA DRIED TOMATO PRODUCTS)

DRIED TOMATO TAPENADE

(See SONOMA DRIED TOMATO PRODUCTS)

GOURMET SAUCE

(See MAKER'S MARK GOURMET SAUCE)

GRAPE LEAVES

Leaves from a grapevine, used as the outer covering in stuffing a variety of fillings: meat, vegetables, and rice, or a combination of all three. Stuffed grape leaves are usually considered Middle Eastern and Greek cuisine.

Grape leaves can be purchased from grocery stores, specialty food stores, and at Middle Eastern groceries. They can also be easily found growing wild during late spring and early summer. The leaves grow in abundance near wooded areas and are best picked by the second week in June as they begin to become bug eaten after that (there will be holes in the leaves). In picking fresh leaves, try to pick the leaves that are nicely green, uniform in size, and void of holes. If you are going to use the leaves right away, wash them thoroughly and parboil in lightly salted water for several minutes. If you plan on freezing the leaves for future use (I keep enough leaves frozen for winter), follow these directions:

Wash freshly picked leaves thoroughly. Place in stacks of 30–35. Roll leaves while they still remain in stacks and tie them with heavy string (do not use twine or yarn), leaving long ends. Boil a large pot of water; add 2 tablespoons of salt. When water comes to a rapid boil, place rolled leaves in the water holding the string ends for several minutes. Remove leaves and drain; squeeze out excess water. Place rolls of leaves in individual plastic bags and freeze. When you are ready to use the frozen leaves: remove the desired amount of rolled leaves from the freezer, soak them in a hot water bath (plug up the kitchen sink), drain the leaves, and prepare to use.

GRAPEFRUIT MARMALADE

Marmalade made with grapefruit. This unusual marmalade can be purchased from some grocery stores or specialty gourmet shops.

GREY OWL WILD RICE

This organically grown rice grows naturally in the crystal clear lakes and streams of northern Canada. Grey Owl wild rice can be found in many local grocery stores, gourmet food shops, or shipped directly from:

> Grey Owl Foods
> P. O. Box 88
> Grand Rapids, MN 55744
> 1-800-527-0172

HERBS

(See RAFAL SPICE COMPANY)

JERK SEASONING

Jerk seasoning is a combination of spices: sweet, spicy-hot, and complex. This seasoning is associated with the Caribbean. Although the jerk sensation has arrived here in the United States, premade is still not always easy to find. Some grocery stores and specialty gourmet shops carry it. I have developed my own recipe after tasting a small portion of jerk seasoning sprinkled on a fruit salad seven years ago in Florida.

Making jerk seasoning: makes ¾ cup—make in small batches
(shelf life is approximately one month)
- 2 teaspoons allspice (Jamaican pimento)
- 2 teaspoons Syrian allspice
- 3 teaspoons dried chili pepper flakes
- 1 teaspoon cayenne pepper
- 4 teaspoons dried chives

1   teaspoon ground cinnamon
1   teaspoon ground coriander seed
1   tablespoon sea salt
2   teaspoons marjoram
1   teaspoon ground ginger
1   tablespoon dried onion flakes
2   tablespoons sugar
2   teaspoons dried lemon grass
2   teaspoons dried thyme

Grind all ingredients together in a food processor, using the steel S blade. Store in a glass jar with a secure lid to retain freshness.

JICAMA

A tuber grown from a tropical vine (sometimes called a Mexican potato) with a flavor closely resembling the water chestnut with a sweeter taste. This deliciously crunchy root vegetable can be eaten raw or cooked, and can be found in the produce section of upscale grocery stores.

JUICE, LIME

(See LIME JUICE, SWEETENED)

KITCHEN GLAMOR

All the kitchen needs of any cook.
Kitchen Glamor
26770 Grand River Avenue
Redford Township, MI 48240
(Main offices and warehouse)
1-313-537-1300
1-313-537-0111 FAX

KITCHEN NEEDS

(See KITCHEN GLAMOR)
(See WILLIAMS-SONOMA)

KITCHEN WARE

(See LE CREUSET—Enameled Cast Iron Cookware from France)
(See KITCHEN GLAMOR—Kitchen Needs)
(See WILLIAMS-SONOMA)

LABAN (LABNE, LEBAN, LEBNE)

Heavy strained yogurt—Middle Eastern yogurt spread. To make laban from low-fat yogurt: Place plain low-fat or no-fat yogurt in either a commercial yogurt strainer or a colander lined with two layers of cheesecloth secured to the inside. Place a large plate beneath the strainer or colander to catch the liquid. Place in the refrigerator for 12–24 hours or until yogurt is thick (sour cream consistency) or cheeselike. Discard the liquid. Laban can be purchased at many grocery stores, Middle Eastern food stores, or gourmet food shops. Keep in mind that prepared laban from the store is quite a bit higher in fat than that prepared at home.

LE CREUSET

Enameled cast iron cookware from France. Warrantied for 101 years from the date of purchase, this outstanding cookware absorbs the heat quickly and distributes it evenly across the cooking surface. Le Creuset can be used on gas, electric, or ceramic top ranges, as well as in conventional ovens. This attractive, colorful cookware is also dishwasher safe.

Call for local suppliers or or further information:

Le Creuset of America, Inc.

in South Carolina

1-803-589-6211

or Le Creuset can be found in kitchen specialty shops, such as:

Kitchen Glamor, Inc.   Williams-Sonoma
26770 Grand River Avenue   100 North Point Street
Redford Township, MI 48240   San Francisco, CA 94133
(Main offices and warehouse)   BY SPECIAL ORDER ONLY
1-313-537-1300   1-415-421-7900
1-313-0111 FAX

LIME JUICE, SWEETENED

Presweetened lime juice used in mixed drinks, flavoring for sparkling water, salad dressings, and marinades. Can be purchased in many grocery stores, liquor stores, and gourmet food shops.

LITE COCONUT MILK

(See COCONUT MILK, LITE)

MAKER'S MARK GOURMET SAUCE

A delicious gourmet sauce for meat, poultry, fish, and vegetables; combines spices and Maker's Mark Bourbon (lots of spices, little bourbon). This sauce can be purchased at some grocery stores, gourmet food shops, or shipped directly from:

Bourbon Country Products, Inc.
4012 Dupont Circle, Suite 304
Louisville, KY 40207
1-800-264-6016

MARMALADE

(See GRAPEFRUIT MARMALADE)

MILK

(See COCONUT MILK, LITE)

MOMBASSA

A hot red pepper powder (hotter than cayenne). (See Mombassa in Spices and Herbs Appendix.) Can be purchased in powder form at Middle Eastern specialty shops, bulk spice specialty stores, or mail ordered from:

Rafal Spice Company
2521 Russell Street
Detroit, MI 48207-2632
1-313-259-6373

MUGWORT—(Use Optionally)

Not generally used in foods, although known to neutralize fat.
(Also see Spices and Herbs Appendix for more information about Mugwort)
Can be purchased at many Oriental markets or mail ordered from:

Rafal Spice Company
2521 Russell Street
Detroit, MI 48207-2632
1-313-259-6373

MUSHROOMS—UNUSUAL MUSHROOMS—DRIED AND FRESH

Dried—an assortment of wild and domestic dried mushrooms are readily available in specialty shops or by mail order from:

Epicurean Specialty
P. O. Box 2209
Sebastopol, CA 95473
1-707-829-3881

Fresh—cremini, oyster, portabello, shiitake
Unusual fresh mushrooms can be purchased at some grocery stores, specialty fruit and vegetable markets, gourmet food shops, or shipped directly from:

Phillips Exotic Mushroom Catalog
909 East Baltimore Pike
Kennett Square, PA 19348
1-215-444-4492

NOODLES

(See SPICY SPIRALS)
(See TOMOSHIRAGA (SOMEN NOODLES))

NUTS

(See PINE NUTS)

ONIONS

(See VIDALIA ONIONS)

ORANGE BLOSSOM WATER

An aromatic combination of orange blossoms and water. This extract and water combination is used primarily in recipes from the Middle East (usually dessert). The taste is sweet and mildly orange. Orange blossom water can be purchased at some grocery stores, Middle Eastern food stores, or gourmet food shops.

OYSTER MUSHROOMS

(See MUSHROOMS—UNUSUAL)

PASTA

(See SPICY SPIRALS)

PEPPERS—ROASTING FRESH PEPPERS OR CHILES.

When purchasing fresh peppers, always choose firm peppers with no wrinkles or marks. Wash the peppers thoroughly and dry with a cloth or paper towel. Use an open gas flame with a rack over it, the outdoor grill, or the broiler. (I place my toaster oven grill on top of my gas burner.) Roast the peppers whole (roast quickly over a hot flame, making sure to blacken the skin without burning the flesh of the pepper). When roasted, place in a glass container and cover with plastic wrap. The peppers will sweat which enhances their flavor as well as gives them time to cool down. Remove the skin with a small knife; the skin should peel easily. Cut off the stems and gently slit the pepper on its side to remove the seeds.

(Also see Chiles in the Spices and Herbs Appendix for more information on various peppers)

PEPPERS—SEEDS FOR PLANTING

Unusual chiles for your garden.

Shepherd's Garden Seeds
6116 Highway 9
Felton, CA 95018-9709
1-408-335-6915

PICKLING SPICE

Pickling spice is a combination of spices used together to infuse flavor in pickling meat, fruits or vegetables, flavoring vinegars, preparing chutneys, marinades or sauces. Depending upon the recipe, you may choose to add the pickling spice loose or as a bouquet garni (in a tea strainer or muslin bag). Pickling spice recipes may include: whole mustard seeds, whole cloves, whole allspice, whole coriander seeds, whole white and black peppercorns, crushed bay leaves, red or dried chili peppers, dill seeds, mace, cardamom pods or seeds, and broken cinnamon quills (or slivered cinnamon bark).

Pickling spice is obtainable at any grocery store. If you have the ingredients on hand, you may wish to make it yourself. (Individually bottled, it makes a nice gift!)

Making my recipe for pickling spice:

2½	ounces mustard seeds
1	ounce whole cloves
3	ounces whole allspice
1	ounce whole coriander seeds
2½	ounces black peppercorns
6	crushed bay leaves
2	ounces dried red peppers
1	teaspoon dill seeds
1½	ounces cardamom seeds

PIGNOLIAS

(See PINE NUTS)

PINE NUTS (PIGNOLAS)

Pine nuts can be purchased from most grocery stores, shops that specialize in assorted nuts, or Middle Eastern food stores.

PORTABELLO MUSHROOMS

(See MUSHROOMS—UNUSUAL)

POTASSIUM NITRATE (SALTPETER)

A fine ground, soluble, crystalline salt used in curing meat. Potassium nitrate can be purchased through local pharmacies.

RADISH

(See DAIKON RADISH)

RAFAL SPICE COMPANY

Spices, teas, coffees, and food specialties, located in Detroit's Eastern Market, it is run like an old world apothecary—spices and herbs weighed out by the owner, Don Rafal and given to the customer in small brown labeled paper bags. Will mail order:
Rafal Spice Company
2521 Russell Street
Detroit, MI 48207-2632
1-313-259-6373

RICE

(See BASMATI RICE)
(See WEHANI RICE)

RICE, WILD

(See GREY OWL WILD RICE)

ROASTING PEPPERS

(See PEPPERS—ROASTING INSTRUCTIONS)

SALTPETER

(See POTASSIUM NITRATE)

SAUCE, GOURMET

(See MAKER'S MARK GOURMET SAUCE)

SAUCE, TOMATO

(See DEI FRATELLI TOMATO SAUCE)

SEEDS, PEPPER

(See PEPPERS—SEEDS FOR PLANTING)

SEEDS, VARIED

(See PEPPERS—SEEDS FOR PLANTING)

SHIITAKE MUSHROOMS

(See MUSHROOMS—UNUSUAL)

SOMEN NOODLES

(See TOMOSHIRAGA—SOMEN NOODLES)

SONOMA DRIED TOMATO PRODUCTS

Products made from sun-dried tomatoes—such as dried tomato bits, tapenade, etc. These delicious sun-dried tomato products can be purchased from some grocery stores, specialty shops, or directly from:

    Timber Crest Farms
    4791 Dry Creek Road
    Healdsburg, CA 95448
      1-707-433-8251

SPICES AND HERBS

(See RAFAL SPICE COMPANY)

SPICY SPIRALS

An unusual pasta made with tomato, cayenne pepper, and basil—pleasantly hot!! This pasta can be purchased at some grocery stores, specialty food shops, or you can call the following direct to tell you the closest location where their product can be purchased:

    A. Zerega's Sons, Inc.   THEY ANSWER EACH
    Antoine's Past   AND EVERY CALL
    P. O. Box 241   1-201-797-1400
    Fair Lawn, NJ 07410

SPINACH POWDER

Fine-ground green powdered spinach; dark green in color; tastes like the vegetable. Can be purchased at:

> Rafal Spice Company
> 2521 Russell Street
> Detroit, MI 48207-2632
> 1-313-259-6373

STRAWBERRY WINE VINEGAR

Strawberry wine vinegar is a light, mild strawberry-flavored wine vinegar. This wine vinegar can be purchased from specialty gourmet food shops or shipped directly from:

> Crabtree & Evelyn, Ltd.
> Peake Brook Road
> Woodstock, CT 06281
> 1-800-624-5211

SWEETENED LIME JUICE

(See LIME JUICE, SWEETENED)

SUN-DRIED TOMATO PRODUCTS

(See SONOMA DRIED TOMATO PRODUCTS)

SYRIAN ALLSPICE

Syrian allspice is a combination of spices with the emphasis on allspice. It is hot and peppery with a sweetness that is subtle and interesting.

Making Syrian allspice:

> (makes ½ pound—stores well)

4	tablespoons pepper
2	tablespoons cayenne pepper
2	tablespoons ground cinnamon
2	tablespoons ground cardamom
4	tablespoons ground cumin
2	tablespoons ground cloves
4	tablespoons ground coriander seed
6	tablespoons ground allspice (Jamaican pimento)
2	tablespoons ground nutmeg
1	tablespoon ground ginger
2	teaspoons rosebud powder (optional)

Grind all ingredients together in a food processor, using the steel S blade. Store in a glass jar with a secure lid to retain freshness.

TAPENADE

(See SONOMA DRIED TOMATO PRODUCTS)

TEA

(See BEEF TEA)
(See CHICKEN TEA)

TOMATO PRODUCTS

(See DEI FRATELLI TOMATO SAUCE AND SEASONED DICED TOMATOES)
(See SONOMA DRIED TOMATO PRODUCTS)

TOMATO SAUCE

(See DEI FRATELLI TOMATO SAUCE)

(TOMATOES

(See DEI FRATELLI SEASONED DICED TOMATOES)
(See SONOMA DRIED TOMATO PRODUCTS)

TOMOSHIRAGA (SOMEN NOODLES)

An Asian noodle made with no cholesterol; light, thin, and beautifully packaged. Somen noodles can be purchased in the Oriental food sections of many grocery stores or from Asian markets.

VIDALIA ONIONS

A delicious, sweet onion from Georgia, usually available at specific times of the year. Vidalia onions can be purchased at some grocery stores, specialty fruit and vegetable markets (at certain times of the year), or shipped directly from:

Bland Farms
P. O. Box 506
Glennville, GA 30427
1-912-654-3048 or
1-800-843-2542

VINEGAR

(See CRANBERRY WINE VINEGAR)
(See STRAWBERRY WINE VINEGAR)

WATER

(See ORANGE BLOSSOM WATER)

WILD RICE

(See GREY OWL WILD RICE)

WILLIAMS-SONOMA

A perfect one-stop shopping for the serious cook with every kitchen need including special yeast (such as Levure Seche de Boulanger/Levure Seche de Saf-Instant, reliable and foolproof Dry Baker's Yeast made in France). Located in many cities throughout the United States or by mail order:

Williams-Sonoma
100 North Point Street
San Francisco, CA 94133
1-415-421-7900

(Also see LE CREUSET for cookware information)

WINE VINEGAR

(See CRANBERRY WINE VINEGAR)
(See STRAWBERRY WINE VINEGAR)

YEAST

For reliable, foolproof dry baker's yeast(s) try:
Levure Seche de Boulanger, Levure Seche de Saf-Instant (made in France)
SAF Products
1-800-641-4615

(See WILLIAMS-SONOMA for source information)

YOGURT—HEAVY STRAINED

(See LABAN)

YOGURT—MIDDLE EASTERN

(See LABAN)

DIETARY
CONCERNS

American Heart Association statistics indicate that over 70 million Americans have some form of cardiovascular disease (this figure indicates a higher than one-in-four ratio for the American public). Over 1.5 million Americans each year will experience a heart attack and, within that number, more than one-half million will not survive. Cardiovascular disease remains the number-one cause of death in the United States.

We have been told there is a link between fat and coronary artery disease, a connection between fat and some cancers, a relationship between fat and high blood pressure, a coupling between fat and liver/kidney disease—are we getting the message? I think not!

Still Americans fill their diets with fats and fatty foods regardless of the media explosion and compulsion for dieting, body conditioning, maintaining an ideal weight, and exercising. Americans have a high incidence of obesity, coronary artery disease, and other fat-related illnesses.

The tides seem to be turning away from labeling cholesterol as the true culprit in coronary artery disease and turning to fat and genetics as the major cause. Cholesterol intake should continue to be monitored, but focus on fat as the real enemy.

Correlations exist between fat and coronary artery disease, hypertension, and cancer. However, pre-existing medical conditions, smoking, and stress are all additional factors in these diseases. Still, it is logical to deduce that if we reduce the amount of fats in our blood by eating a low-fat diet, we may avoid and even decrease the risk of fat-related diseases.

The American Heart Association suggests that the total intake of dietary fat should be 30 percent or less of total daily caloric intake. Of this 30 percent, less than 10 percent should be saturated fat with the majority being mono or polyunsaturated fats. These numbers are based on a weight-maintenance diet, and even more stringent fat limits are required for weight-reduction diets. Many experts in the field of nutrition and dietary concerns are pushing these numbers back to a 20 percent total. It is important to keep in mind that these guidelines are not intended or recommended for children.

Cholesterol is an animal fat not found in vegetable oils, but present in all meat and animal products. Daily intake of cholesterol should be kept under 300 mg per day.

Fats are made up of substances called fatty acids. Essential fatty acids are not manufactured within our bodies and must be included into our diets as they provide the foundation for membranes that develop the outer borders of body cells.

Lipids combine with proteins to form water-soluble lipoproteins. These lipoproteins are responsible for transporting fats through the blood from organ to organ. Some lipoproteins, for instance LDL, lead to the accumulation of fatty plaque within the blood vessel wall. This leads to coronary artery disease.

We've all heard the terms LDL and HDL in relationship to cholesterol. LDL (low-density lipoprotein—fat that adheres to the lining of the arteries and causes blockage) is the bad cholesterol and HDL (high-density lipoprotein—which fights against the fat build up and removes the deposits of cholesterol that adhere to the insides of arteries) is the good cholesterol.

Triglycerides are the body's main storage form of fat (and calories) and consist of three (3) fatty acids and a glycerol molecule (a carbohydrate, like sugar). Triglycerides are produced and transported from the liver and are metabolized in other organs such as muscle and fat. Blood triglycerides represent not only the production and secretion of triglycerides by the liver (VLDL) but levels also rise after fat ingestion. Because triglycerides are produced by the liver, a low-fat diet alone may not affect the triglyceride level. Fat does have more than twice the calories per gram than proteins and starches; therefore, a reduction of fat is certainly a major source in reduction of calories, but it is not inclusive of other caloric changes that add additional calories.

Our bodies, with no added help, produce cholesterol. By adding too much fat to our diets, we are elevating our risk of illness or death. Low-fat, low-cholesterol diets abate circulating cholesterol by altering its metabolism in the liver and thus enabling the liver to remove the cholesterol from the bloodstream. There are many individuals who monitor their diet closely, exercise, and do all of the correct things to maintain an appropriate cholesterol level—still, their levels are high.

This grouping may have to consider medication to keep their cholesterol levels within normal range.

We hear the terms saturated, polyunsaturated, and monounsaturated fats over and over again—what exactly do they mean? Saturated fats raise blood cholesterol levels. These fats include those that are solid at room temperature and those coming from animal sources (dairy and meat) as well as tropical oils (palm and coconut).

Unsaturated fats tend to lower blood cholesterol levels. These fats tend to be liquid at room temperature and are found in vegetable and fish oils. While polyunsaturated fats tend to lower both LDL and HDL, monounsaturated fats have been shown to mainly reduce LDL and either have no effect on HDL or raise it—increasing the HDL/LDL ratio.

Trans fatty acids are a special type of unsaturated fat. With the push toward unsaturated fats for better health, many food producers are including trans fatty acids in their products, as there is a chemical similarity to saturated fats. Unfortunately, along with their beneficial properties for the food industry, they also share the tendency to raise blood cholesterol. Many questions still exist about specific trans fatty acids and their effects. Because food producers are not required to reveal the amount of trans fatty acids in their products—we, as consumers, need to look at these as a potential "red flag."

Hydrogenation is the chemical process in which hydrogen atoms are added to an unsaturated fat in order to form a saturated fat. Companies hydrogenate fat to reduce the likelihood of its becoming rancid, to give it more longevity in re-use for frying, to increase taste, and to make the oils in margarine more spreadable. Saturated fats raise blood cholesterol and should be avoided. Partially hydrogenated fats tend to be a mixture of polyunsaturated, monounsaturated, and saturated fats. Hydrogenation changes some of the polyunsaturated fat into trans fatty acids, which raise cholesterol levels. Some foods are totally hydrogenated and should be considered saturated fats.

In purchasing oils and prepared food products, carefully read the labels. Buyer beware—there is a significant difference between products and many tricks in labeling. Many foods will advertise 100 percent pure vegetable oil—no cholesterol, when in fact there was no cholesterol in vegetable products to begin with. Only, in the fine print, you may find that the unsaturated fat used has been hydrogenated and is therefore no longer an unsaturated fat. Always look for products that have the highest percentage of unsaturated and or monounsaturated fats possible. Remember, the less solid oils are at room temperature, the safer they are for your body.

In 1990 the Congressional Nutrition Labeling and Education Act was passed. This goaded the FDA (Food and Drug Administration) to join forces with the USDA (United States Department of Agriculture) to set more stringent regulations for food labeling. In 1991 the most compendious food labeling regulations of all time were mandated. Additional restrictions were imposed in January of 1993, and the guidelines for 1995 are the most stringent as disclosures of nutritional information on certain food products will be mandatory rather than voluntary.

Regardless of these new regulations, labels can still be misleading and difficult to understand. Take the time to acquaint yourself with some of the jargon necessary to understand what the charts and listings mean. If a food producer voluntarily labels the monounsaturated and polyunsaturated fats on a product, you can estimate the amount of trans fatty acids by simply subtracting the saturated, polyunsaturated, and monounsaturated fats from the total fat grams listed. Many labels do not disclose the amount of monounsaturated fat, making it impossible to determine how much of the unlisted fat is in that category and how much are trans fatty acids.

Although fats contain at least 9 calories per gram—when concerned with lowering LDL cholesterol, do not focus only on caloric counts; concentrate on the words polyunsaturated and monounsaturated.

In this cookbook, the only oils used are canola and light olive oil. Both are monounsaturated fats and both appear to have benefits on our body's LDL/HDL ratio.

A generic guideline for adult daily fat consumption is: take your total amount of calories for the day and multiply them by .30 and divide by 9. Keep the fat below 30 percent of your total daily intake.

Total amount of calories x .30 for the day

9

NUTRIENT COMPOSITION OF BISON

by Martin J. Marchello, Ph.D., Professor, North Dakota State University, Department of Animal and Range Sciences, College of Agriculture

Consumers are presently expressing concern over the nutrient composition of their diets. The nutritional value of foods depends on nutrient content and availability, quantity eaten, and the composition of the total diet. The livelihood of Native Americans and even early settlers required the harvest of game for food. The role of game meats as a source of food has been largely ignored in modern times, yet they may provide the principle meat source for many individuals in the United States as well as in some developing countries.

Bison (buffalo) meat has seen a recent increase in consumer demand because it is perceived as a source of healthful, lean red meat. Bison has less intramuscular fat (marbling) and less carcass fat thus producing more lean red meat than beef. Bison is a highly nutrient-dense food because of the proportion of protein, fat, minerals, and vitamins to its caloric value.

Table 1 shows the nutrient content of lean domestic and game meats. Bison compares favorably with the other meats analyzed. It has 74.5 percent moisture with 21.7 percent protein and 1.9 percent fat. With a cholesterol content of 62 mg per 100 grams (3.5 ounces) it is as low in cholesterol as any other meats except wild turkey. The combination of lean meat and low fat gives bison a caloric value of 138 kilocalories per 100 grams (3.5 ounces). The mineral content of various domestic and game animals is shown in Table 2. Bison compares favorably with the other animals studied. It is low in sodium, higher in iron and intermediate in zinc content compared to domestic meats. Bison is a good source of various minerals necessary for human health.

The relative percentages of selected fatty acids of lean meat of various mammalian species is shown in Table 3. Bison contains greater amounts of unsaturated fats (fatty acids) than beef. Individual fatty acids vary considerably. The ratio of stearic to palmitic acid in bison is worthy of note.

Recent studies indicate that palmitic acid may be involved in raising human serum cholesterol and that stearic acid may lower serum cholesterol. These data show that bison has a lower palmitic to stearic acid ratio compared to beef suggesting that bison meat may have a positive effect on serum cholesterol. More research needs to be done in this area in order to draw definitive conclusions.

The preceding information is based on research conducted on raw meat because this is the way consumers purchase meat. Data drawn from raw meat research is more consistent because cooking methods and end point temperatures vary considerably. However, we consume cooked meat. Only limited data is available (Table 4) on the nutrient composition of cooked bison. In general, cooking tends to reduce moisture content of meat concentrating the nutrients. For instance, the same quantity of meat (3.5 ounces) which when analyzed raw contains 21.7 grams of protein, contains 32.7 grams protein (and approximately 3.0 ounces) after cooking. The amount of protein has not increased absolutely, but is higher in relation to the weight of the meat after cooking.

Each individual's ability to absorb and metabolize nutrients varies and this data should not be construed as the solution to medical problems associated with diet. This information should help you make decisions about the role of meat in your diet. Bison compares very favorably with domestic meats and is a healthy option for those who enjoy red meat.

REFERENCES

Cox, B. L. 1978. "Comparison of meat quality from bison and beef cattle." B.S. Thesis. University of Saskatchewan, Saskatoon.

Koch, R. M., J. D. Crouse and S. C. Seideman. 1987. "Bison, Brahman and Hereford carcass characteristics." Abstract. *Amer. Soc. Animal Sci.* (Midwestern Section), p. 124.

Marchello, M. J., W. D. Slanger, D. B. Milne, H. G. Fischer and P. T. Berg. 1989. "Nutrient composition of raw and cooked bison." *J. Food Comp. and Analysis.* 2:177-185.

Anderson, B. B. 1989. "Composition of Foods." *USDA Handbook* 8-17. U.S. Department of Agriculture, Washington, D.C.

SUGGESTED READINGS

Allen, J. A. (Joel Asaph), (1838-1921), *History of the American Bison, Bison Americanus,* Washington, Government Printing Office, 1877.

Amory, Cleveland, et al., *The American Heritage Cookbook and Illustrated History of American Eating and Drinking,* Edited by American Heritage, The Magazine of History, (City and State Unlisted), American Heritage Publishing Co., Inc., 1964.

Bakeless, John, *Lewis & Clark: Partners in Discovery,* New York, William Morrow & Company, 1947.

Blackstone, Sarah J. (1954-), *Buckskins, Bullets, and Business: A History of Buffalo Bill's Wild West,* Westport, Conneticut, Greenwood Press, 1986.

Bonar, Ann, *The Macmillan Treasury of Herbs: A Complete Guide to the Cultivation and Use of Wild and Domesticated Herbs,* New York, New York, Macmillan Publishing Company, 1985.

Carr, Anna, et al., *Rodale's Illustrated Encyclopedia of Herbs,* Edited by Claire Kowalchik & William H. Hylton, Emmaus, Pennsylvania, Rodale Press, Inc., 1987.

Dary, David A., *The Buffalo Book: The Full Saga of the American Animal,* (Sage Books), Chicago, Illinois, The Swallow Press Incorporated, 1974.

Duke, P. G., *Points in Time: Structure and Event in a Late Northern Plains Hunting Society,* Niwot, Colorado, University Press of Colorado, 1991.

Garretson, Martin S., *The American Bison: The Story of its Extermination as a Wild Species and its Restoration under Federal Protection,* New York, New York Zoological Society, 1938.

Grissom, Abigail W., "Food Under Scrutiny," *Academic Inter-national Encyclopedia,* (1992 Health and Medicine), United States of America, Lexicon Publications, Inc., pgs. 223-227, 1992.

Irwin, Stephen, *The Indian Hunters,* Hancock House Publishers, Blaine, WA, 1984

————, *Hunters of the Buffalo,* Hancock House Publishers, Blaine, WA, 1984.

Meagher, Margaret Mary, *The Bison of Yellowstone National Park,* Washington, United States National Park Services, may be purchased from the Superintendent of Documents, Government Printing Office, 1973.

National Buffalo Association, *Buffalo Producer's Guide to Management & Marketing,* edited by Kim Dowling, Chicago, Illinois, R. R. Donnelley & Sons Company, 1990.

Norman, Jill, *The Complete Book of Spices: A Practical Guide to Spices & Aromatic Seeds,* New York, New York, Viking Penguin, 1991.

Roe, Frank Gilbert, *The North American Buffalo: A Critical Study of the Species in its Wild State,* Toronto, Canada, University of Toronto Press, 1951.

Sandoz, Mari (1896-1966), *The Buffalo Hunters; The Story of the Hide Men,* New York, Hastings House, 1954.

Thomas, Dave and Karin Ronnefeldt (Edited by), *People of the First Man: Life Among the Plains Indians in Their Final Days of Glory,* New York, New York, Promontory Press, 1982.

Table 1. Nutrient Content of Lean* Domestic and Game Meats

	Moisture (g/ 100g)	Protein (g/ 100g)	Fat (g/ 100g)	Choles- terol (mg/ 100g)	Energy* (Kcal/ 100g)
Beef (USDA Choice)	70.2	22.0	6.5	72	180
Beef (USDA STD)	73.2	22.7	2.0	69	152
Pork	71.9	22.3	4.9	71	165
Lamb***	73.2	20.8	5.7	66	167
Buffalo/Bison	74.5	21.7	1.9	62	138
Whitetail Deer	73.5	23.6	1.4	116	149
Mule Deer	73.4	23.7	1.3	107	145
Elk	74.8	22.8	0.9	67	137
Moose	75.8	22.1	0.5	71	130
Antelope	73.9	22.5	0.9	112	144
Squirrel	73.8	21.4	3.2	83	149
Cottontail	74.5	21.8	2.4	77	144
Jackrabbit	73.8	21.9	2.4	131	153
Chicken	75.7	23.6	0.7	62	135
Turkey	73.8	23.5	1.5	60	146
Wild Turkey	71.7	25.7	1.1	55	163
Pheasant (Domestic)	74.0	23.9	0.8	71	144
Wild Pheasant	72.4	25.7	0.6	52	148
Grey Partridge	72.1	25.6	0.7	85	151
Sharptail Grouse	74.2	23.8	0.7	105	142
Sage Grouse	74.3	23.7	1.1	101	140
Dove	73.6	22.9	1.8	94	145
Sandhill Crane	73.2	21.7	2.4	123	153
Snow Goose	71.1	22.7	3.6	142	121
Mallard	73.2	23.1	2.0	140	152
Widgeon	73.5	22.6	2.1	131	153

* Mammal Samples—Longissimus Muscle and Avian Samples—Breast Muscle
** Determined by bomb calorimeter
*** Results of research conducted at North Dakota State University. All values (except lamb which is published in *The Journal of Food Science*) are the result of original research at North Dakota State University. Some of these results have been published.

Table 2. Mineral Content of Lean Tissue from Domestic & Game Meats*

Species	Mineral (mg/100g)								
	K	P	Na	Ca	Cu	Fe	Mg	Mn	Zn
Lamb	276	190	68	12.	.128	1.91	27	.024	3.19
Pork	420	204	52	4.4	.17	0.8	25	.028	1.5
Beef	366	172	52	4.2	.13	1.8	23	.013	3.4
Buffalo/Bison	315	177	52	5.5	.07	2.5	23	.003	2.4
Mule Deer	305	166	54	3.3	.14	2.7	25	.017	1.4
Whitetail Deer	284	212	51	3.8	.28	3.6	23	.041	2.0
Elk	312	161	58	3.8	.12	2.7	23	.012	2.4
Antelope	339	180	49	3.2	.17	3.1	26	.019	1.2
Moose	316	149	65	3.6	.07	3.0	22	.008	2.8
Chicken	297	180	42	4.7	.013	0.6	28	.002	0.52
Pheasant	334	219	50	5.1	.039	1.2	32	.048	0.64
Sharptail Grouse	279	200	67	7.2	.26	4.8	29	.04	0.73
Sage Grouse	349	226	57	5.3	.21	4.1	31	.035	0.71
Grey Partridge	364	223	43	4.7	.17	2.7	32	.031	0.66
Dove	323	252	64	5.3	.32	4.3	31	.043	0.64

* Mammal Samples—Longissimus Muscle and Avian Samples—Breast Muscle
+ Results of research conducted at North Dakota University

Table 3.   Fatty Acid Profiles of Longissimus Muscle
from Various Mammalian Species

Fatty Acid	Beef	Bison/ Buffalo	Mule Deer	Whitetail Deer	Elk	Antel- ope	Moose
N	(30)	(20)	(29)	(21)	(21)	(23)	(25)
			Relative Percentage				
Myristic	2.7	1.2	1.6	0.82	4.8	0.86	0.47
Myristoleic	0.6	0.42	0.14	0.10	1.6	0.38	0.19
Palmitic	27.9	20.5	21.6	19.0	29.4	17.3	14.5
Palmitoleic	3.3	2.5	1.8	1.5	10.0	1.6	1.2
Stearic	15.7	21.4	24.8	25.8	14.3	23.0	21.6
Oleic	41.6	42.0	29.9	28.9	14.9	25.2	23.0
Linoleic	5.8	6.6	11.6	15.6	14.6	19.1	23.8
Linolenic	0.51	2.0	4.4	2.9	3.4	4.5	4.2
Arachidonic	1.8	3.2	4.2	5.4	7.0	8.1	11.2
Saturated	46.3	43.2	48.0	45.6	48.4	41.2	36.6
Monounsaturated	45.5	45.0	31.8	30.6	26.6	27.1	24.3
Polyunsaturated	8.2	11.8	20.2	23.9	24.9	31.6	39.1

N = numbers of observations

Table 4.   Nutrient Composition of Cooked Lean Meat
from the Loin, Top Round and
Shoulder Muscles of Bison

Nutrient	Loin (10 samples)	Top Round (3 samples)	Shoulder (9 samples)
Moisture %	61.8	63.3	62.8
Protein %	32.7	32.3	31.3
Fat %	4.0	2.4	4.1
Mineral %	1.5	1.5	1.3
Cholesterol (mg/100gm)	108.0	136.0	110.0
Energy (kcal/100gm)	212.0	200.0	213.0

▲▲▲▲▲▲▲▲▲▲◆▲▲▲▲▲▲▲▲▲▲

Depending of course, on the way in which it is prepared, buffalo meat can be a delicious, healthy alternative to a variety of foods. It is lower in calories, fat, and cholesterol than beef or chicken, and makes a wonderful, nutritious addition to any meal. Try substituting buffalo for beef or chicken in old favorites or create new recipes of your own.

Florine Mark, President & CEO, The W W Group, Inc., (largest franchise of Weight Watchers Int'l.)

BUFFALO MEAT COMPARISON
3½ ounce cooked portions

	Cal.	Fat	Chol.	Iron
BEEF				
broiled, top loin	207	9.4 g	76 mg	5.0 mg
CHICKEN				
roasted, light meat	173	4.5 g	85 mg	1.0 mg
VENISON	158	3.2 g	112 mg	3.5 mg
BUFFALO				
roasted	130	2.0 g	61 mg	2.0 mg

Florine Mark, President & CEO, The W W Group, Inc., (Largest franchise of Weight Watchers Int'l.)

When comparing the fat content of different species of animals, there is a great variance in the amount of fat between species.
When comparing cholesterol of different species of animals, there is very little variance in the cholesterol content between species.

Calories, Protein, Lipid, and Cholesterol in 100 grams of Meat of Various Species

Food:	Raw				Cooked				
	Calories	Protein	Lipid Fat	Cholesterol	Cooking Method	Calories	Protein	Lipid Fat	Cholesterol
		g	g	mg			g	g	mg
Domesticated animal meats Composite of retail cuts:									
Beef 1									
lean only	144	20.78	6.16	59	cooked	216	29.58	9.91	86
lean & fat, 1/4" fat trim	251	18.24	19.24	67	cooked	305	25.94	21.54	88
Pork 2									
lean only	143	21.07	5.88	61	cooked	212	29.27	9.66	86
lean & fat	216	18.95	14.95	67	cooked	273	27.57	17.18	91
Lamb 3, choice grade									
lean	134	20.29	5.25	65	cooked	206	28.22	9.52	92
lean & fat	267	16.88	21.59	72	cooked	294	24.52	20.94	97
Veal 3									
lean	112	20.20	2.87	83	cooked	196	31.90	6.58	118
lean & fat	144	19.35	6.77	82	cooked	231	30.10	11.39	114
Rabbit 3, domesticated									
composite of cuts	136	20.05	5.55	57	roasted	197	29.06	8.05	82
composite of cuts					stewed	206	30.38	8.41	86
Chicken 4									
meat only	119	21.39	3.08	70	roasted	190	28.93	7.41	84
meat & skin	215	18.60	15.06	75	roasted	239	27.30	13.60	88
Turkey 4									
meat only	119	21.77	2.86	65	roasted	170	29.32	4.97	76
meat & skin	160	20.42	8.02	68	roasted	208	28.10	9.73	82
Game Meats 3									
Antelope	114	22.38	2.03	95	roasted	150	29.45	2.67	126
Bear	161	20.10	8.30	—	simmered	259	32.42	13.39	—
Beaver	146	24.05	4.80	—	roasted	166	27.33	5.45	—
Beefalo	143	23.30	4.80	44	roasted	188	30.66	6.32	58
Bison	109	21.62	1.84	62	roasted	143	28.44	2.42	82
Boar, wild	122	21.51	3.33	—	roasted	160	28.30	4.38	—
Buffalo, water	99	20.39	1.37	46	roasted	131	26.83	1.80	61
Caribou	127	22.63	3.36	83	roasted	167	29.77	4.42	109
Deer	120	22.96	2.42	85	roasted	158	30.21	3.19	112
Elk	111	22.95	1.45	55	roasted	146	30.19	1.90	73
Goat	109	20.60	2.31	57	roasted	143	27.10	3.03	75
Horse	133	21.39	4.60	52	roasted	175	28.14	6.05	68
Moose	102	22.24	0.74	59	roasted	134	29.27	0.97	78
Muskrat	162	20.76	8.10	—	roasted	184	23.59	9.20	—
Opossum					roasted	221	30.20	10.20	—
Rabbit, wild	114	21.79	2.32	81	stewed	173	33.02	3.51	123
Raccoon					roasted	255	29.20	14.50	—
Squirrel	120	21.23	3.21	83	roasted	136	24.13	3.65	95

1 *Agriculture Handbook* No. 8-13, Beef Products, 1990
2 *Agriculture Handbook* No. 8-10, Pork Products, in press
3 *Agriculture Handbook* No. 8-17, Lamb, Veal, Game Products, 1989
4 *Agriculture Handbook* No. 8- 5, Poultry Products, 1979
  June 1, 1992

Nutrients and Units	Amount in 100 grams, edible portion			Amount in edible portion of common measures of food	
	Mean	Stan-dard error	No. of Sam-ples	Approximate measure & weight 1 oz. = 28.4 g	1 lb. = 453.6 g
(A)	(B)	(C)	(D)	(E)	(F)
Proximate:					
Water . . . . g	74.57	0.259	33	21.18	337.52
kcal	109.			31.	493.
Food energy . . . . kj	456.			129.	2,063.
Protein (N x6.25) . . . . . g	21.62	0.164	33	6.14	97.84
Total lipid (fat) . . . . g	1.84	0.158	33	0.52	8.31
Carbohydrate, total . . . . g	0.00			0.00	0.00
Crude fiber . . . . g					
Ash . . . . g	1.20	0.037	33	0.34	5.43
Minerals:					
Calcium . . . . mg	6.	0.240	23	2.	27.
Iron . . . . mg	2.6	0.060	30	0.74	11.77
Magnesium . . . . . . mg	25.	0.329	30	7.	113.
Phosphorus . . . . . . mg	187.	2.611	30	53.	846.
Potassium . . . . mg	343.	5.295	30	97.	1,552.
Sodium . . . . mg	54.	0.913	30	15.	244.
Zinc . . . . mg	2.80	0.069	30	0.80	12.67
Copper . . . . mg	0.090	0.010	30	0.026	0.407
Manganese . . . . . . mg	0.007	0.000	30	0.002	0.032
Vitamins:					
Asorbic acid . . . . . . mg					
Thiamin . . . . mg					
Riboflavin . . . . mg					
Niacin . . . . mg					
Pantothenic acid . . . . mg					
Vitamin B6 . . . . . . mg					
Folacin . . . . mcg					
Vitamin B12 . . . . . . mcg					
RE					
Vitamin A . . . . }IU					
Lipids:					
Fatty acids:					
Saturated, total . . . . g	0.69			0.20	3.13
4:0 . . . . g					
6:0 . . . . g					
8:0 . . . . g					
10:0 . . . . g					
12:0 . . . . g					
14:0 . . . . g	0.02		22	0.01	0.09
16:0 . . . . g	0.33		22	0.09	1.48
18:0 . . . . g	0.35		22	0.10	1.56
Monounsaturated, total . . . . g	0.72			0.20	3.26
16:1 . . . . g	0.04		22	0.01	0.19
18:1 . . . . g	0.67		22	0.19	3.04
20:1 . . . . g					
22:1 . . . . g					

GAME MEAT, Bison, Raw

Nutrients and Units	Amount in 100 grams, edible portion			Amount in edible portion of common measures of food	
	Mean	Standard error	No. of Samples	Approximate measure & weight 1 oz. = 28.4 g	1 lb. = 453.6 g
(A)	(B)	(C)	(D)	(E)	(F)
Polyunsaturated,					
total . . . . g	0.19			0.05	0.84
18:2 . . . . g	0.11		22	0.03	0.48
18:3 . . . . g	0.03		22	0.01	0.14
18:4 . . . . g					
20:4 . . . . g	0.05		22	0.01	0.22
20:5 . . . . g					
22:5 . . . . g					
22:6 . . . . g					
Cholesterol* . . . . mg	62.	2.437	50	18.	282.
Phytosterols . . . . mg					
Amino Acids:					
Tryptophan . . . . g					
Threonine . . . . g	0.890		1	0.253	4.030
Isoleucine . . . . g	0.911		1	0.259	4.121
Leucine . . . . g	1.679		1	0.477	7.601
Lysine . . . . g	1.686		1	0.479	7.632
Methionine . . . . g	0.513		1	0.146	2.320
Cystine					
Phenylalanine . . . . . . g	0.809		1	0.230	3.663
Tyrosine . . . . g	0.695		1	0.197	3.144
Valine . . . . g	0.978		1	0.278	4.426
Arginine . . . . g	1.282		1	0.364	5.800
Histidine . . . . g	0.573		1	0.163	2.595
Alanine . . . . g	1.228		1	0.349	5.556
Aspartic acid . . . . g	1.875		1	0.533	8.487
Glutamic acid . . . . g	3.150		1	0.895	14.256
Glycine . . . . g	1.039		1	0.295	4.701
Proline . . . . g	0.863		1	0.245	3.907
Serine . . . . g	0.823		1	0.234	3.724

* Range is 36–109 mg per 100 g.

A H—8-17 (1989)
NDB No. 17156

GAME MEAT, Bison, Cooked, Roasted

Nutrients and Units	Amount in 100 grams, edible portion			Amount in edible portion of common measures of food	
	Mean	Stan-dard error	No. of Sam-ples	Approximate measure & weight 1 lb. raw 3 oz. boneless equals 85 g	yields 340 g
(A)	(B)	(C)	(D)	(E)	(F)
Proximate:					
Water . . . . g	66.54			56.56	226.38
kcal	143.			122.	487.
Food energy . . . . }kj	600.			510.	2,040.
Protein (N x6.25) . . . . . g	28.44			24.18	96.77
Total lipid (fat) . . . . . . g	2.42			2.05	8.22
Carbohydrates					
total . . . . g	0.00			0.00	0.00
Crude fiber . . . . g					
Ash . . . . g	1.58			1.34	5.37
Minerals:					
Calcium . . . . mg	8.			7.	26.
Iron . . . . mg	3.42			2.91	11.64
Magnesium . . . . mg	26.			22.	90.
Phosphorus . . . . mg	209.			178.	712.
Potassium . . . . mg	361.			307.	1,228.
Sodium . . . . mg	57.			48.	193.
Zinc . . . . mg	3.68			3.13	12.53
Copper . . . . mg	0.107			0.091	0.363
Manganese . . . . mg	0.008			0.007	0.027
Vitamins:					
Asorbic acid . . . . mg					
Thiamin . . . . mg					
Riboflavin . . . . mg					
Niacin . . . . mg					
Pantothenic acid . . . . mg					
Vitamin B6 . . . . mg					
Folacin . . . . mcg					
Vitamin B12 . . . . mcg					
RE					
Vitamin A . . . . {IU					
Lipids:					
Fatty acids:					
Saturated,					
total . . . . g	0.91			0.77	3.10
4:0 . . . . g					
6:0 . . . . g					
8:0 . . . . g					
10:0 . . . . g					
12:0 . . . . g					
14:0 . . . . g	0.03			0.02	0.09
16:0 . . . . g	0.43			0.37	1.46
18:0 . . . . : . . g	0.45			0.39	1.55
Monounsaturated,					
total . . . . g	0.95			0.80	3.22
16:1 . . . . g	0.06			0.05	0.19
18:1 . . . . g	0.88			0.75	3.00
20:1 . . . . g					
22:1 . . . . g					

GAME MEAT, Bison, Cooked, Roasted

Nutrients and Units	Amount in 100 grams, edible portion			Amount in edible portion of common measures of food	
	Mean	Standard error	No. of Samples	Approximate measure & weight 1 lb. raw 3 oz. boneless equals 85 g	yields 340 g
(A)	(B)	(C)	(D)	(E)	(F)
Polyunsaturated,					
total . . . . g	0.24			0.21	0.83
18:2 . . . . g	0.14			0.12	0.47
18:3 . . . . g	0.04			0.03	0.14
18:4 . . . . g					
20:4 . . . . g	0.07			0.06	0.22
20:5 . . . . g					
22:5 . . . . g					
22:6 . . . . g					
Cholesterol . . . . mg	82.			70.	279.
Phytosterols . . . . mg					
Amino Acids:					
Tryptophan . . . . g					
Threonine . . . . g	1.171			0.996	3.985
Isoleucine . . . . g	1.198			1.018	4.076
Leucine . . . . g	2.210			1.878	7.518
Lysine . . . . g	2.219			1.886	7.548
Methionine . . . . g	0.674			0.573	2.295
Cystine . . . . g					
Phenylalanine . . . . . . g	1.065			0.905	3.623
Tyrosine . . . . g	0.914			0.777	3.110
Valine . . . . g	1.287			1.094	4.378
Arginine . . . . g	1.686			1.433	5.736
Histidine . . . . g	0.754			0.641	2.566
Alanine . . . . g	1.615			1.373	5.495
Aspartic acid . . . . g	2.467			2.097	8.393
Glutamic acid . . . . g	4.145			3.523	14.100
Glycine . . . . g	1.367			1.162	4.650
Proline . . . . g	1.136			0.966	3.865
Serine . . . . g	1.083			0.920	3.683

A H—8-17 (1989)
NDB No. 17156

BISON/BUFFALO
SUPPLIERS

CALIFORNIA

Star B Buffalo Ranch
Ken Childs
28428 Hwy. 78
Ramona, CA 92065
1-619-789-5767
1-619-789-9387 FAX

COLORADO

Denver Buffalo Company
Charles J. Maas
1120 Lincoln Street
Suite 905
Denver, CO 80203
1-800-BUY-BUFF

IOWA

Buffalo Ridge Ranch
Gary Lenz
2685 Kerper Blvd.
Dubuqui, IA 52001
1-319-557-8229

MICHIGAN

Butcher Boy Food Products
Don or Barbara Francis
13869 Herbert Street
Warren, MI 48089
1-313-779-0600

Great Lakes Buffalo Co. Inc.
Brenda Sangster
2690 Riggsville Road
Cheboygan, MI 49721
1-616-627-5418

LeeGrande Ranch
Harry & Madeleine Peterson
1313 M33 Highway
Cheboygan, MI 49721
1-616-238-4546

MISSOURI

Sayersbrook Bison Ranch
Herbert M. "Skip" Sayers or
Thirza Sayers
Route 2, Box 73
Potosi, MO 63664
1-314-438-5054
1-314-968-5400

MONTANA

McBuff Bison
Dr. John McIlhattan
2717 McIlhattan Road
Bozeman, MT 59715
1-406-586-9094

NEW MEXICO

Circle Bar West
Patrick F. Taylor
P.O. Box 337, Hwy. 395,
Silver Bridge Road
Tinnie, NM 88351
1-505-653-4592

NEW YORK

Frontier Buffalo Company
Vern Jackson
395 South End Avenue
Suite 31D
New York, NY 10280
1-212-466-2833

NORTH DAKOTA

North American Bison
Cooperative
Brad Lodge, Manager
RR 1, Box 162B
New Rockford, ND 58356
1-701-947-2505
1-701-947-2105 FAX

PENNSYLVANIA

Juniata Springs Bison Farm
Shirley Drewes
RR 2, Box 1640
Miffintown, PA 17059
1-717-436-9795

Wooden Nickel Buffalo Farm
& Trading Post
Dan and Mickey Koman
5909 Koman Road
Eniboro, PA 16412-1255
1-814-734-BUFF

CANADA

Norton Game Farms Inc.
3805 Oak Drive S.
Lethbridge, Alberta
T1K 4H3
403-329-1766

CONVERSION TABLES FORMULAS FOR METRIC CONVERSION

In early times, Americans bought and measured their food by volume; Europeans weighed their ingredients. Times and ingredients have changed; Americans are no longer using a teacup or wine glass full as a tool of measurement and yet, there still remains a difference in the way Americans and Europeans measure food.

FAHRENHEIT TO CELSIUS (CENTIGRADE), subtract 32 and multiply by 5/9.

CELSIUS (CENTIGRADE) TO FAHRENHEIT, multiply by 915 and add 32.

LIQUID INGREDIENTS/VOLUME

Ounces	Milliliters	Milliliters	Liquid
1	29.57	1	0.03
2	59.15	2	0.07
3	88.72	3	0.10
4	118.30	4	0.14
5	147.87	5	0.17
6	177.44	6	0.20
7	207.02	7	0.24
8	236.59	8	0.27
9	266.16	9	0.30
10	295.73	10	0.33

Quarts	Liters	Liters	Quarts
1	0.95	1	1.06
2	1.89	2	2.11
3	2.84	3	3.17
4	3.79	4	4.23
5	4.73	5	5.28
6	5.68	6	6.34
7	6.62	7	7.40
8	7.57	8	8.45
9	8.52	9	9.51
10	9.47	10	10.57

Gallons	Liters	Liters	Gallons
1	3.78	1	0.26
2	7.57	2	0.53
3	11.36	3	0.79
4	15.14	4	1.06
5	18.93	5	1.32
6	22.71	6	1.59
7	26.50	7	1.85
8	30.28	8	2.11
9	34.07	9	2.38
10	37.86	10	2.74